The World of Upstairs, Downstairs

The World of Upstairs, Downstairs

by Mollie Hardwick

HOLT, RINEHART AND WINSTON

NEW YORK

PHOTO CREDITS

William Gordon Davis, p. 249; Walt Disney Productions, p. 235; Mary Evans Picture Library, pp. 12, 15, 18, 19, 28, 31, 43, 47, 48, 69, 80, 93 (inset), 164, 220 (bottom); Fotomas Index (John Freeman Ltd.), pp. 40, 57; Ronald Grant, pp. 138, 143 (left and right), 158 (left), 182, 188, 189, 192, 195, 200, 201, 203 (left and right), 204, 230 (top), 234, 241; Mollie Hardwick, p. 183; Imperial War Museum, pp. 109, 150, 161, 162, 166, 170 (top and bottom), 171 (left), 173, 176; Kodak Museum, pp. 17, 21, 23, 30, 58–59, 97, 98, 111 (top), 165, 247; London Weekend Television, pp. 27, 36, 45, 65, 74, 82, 85, 95, 99, 108, 115, 116–117, 119, 133, 141, 153, 160, 167, 180, 191, 199, 206, 228, 250; The Raymond Mander and Joe Mitchenson Collection, pp. 132, 145 (top and bottom), 156, 158 (right), 205, 237 (left and right); The Mansell Collection, pp. 22, 29, 32–33, 44, 92–93; Mobil Oil Corp., frontispiece; Popperfoto, pp. 120, 122, 124, 127, 130, 149, 152, 169, 171 (right), 214, 216 (top and bottom), 223, 225, 227; The Radio Times Hulton Picture Library, pp. 20, 24, 35, 38 (top and bottom), 50, 51, 53, 54, 60 (left and right), 62–63, 64, 66–67, 70, 71, 75, 81 (left and right), 86, 88, 90, 94, 100, 101, 106, 107, 109, 110, 111 (bottom), 112, 118, 126, 129, 135, 136, 146, 147, 163 (left), 177, 181, 184, 185, 186, 187, 197, 207, 208, 210, 214, 218, 219, 220 (top), 221, 224, 229, 230 (bottom), 232 (top and bottom), 238 (top left, bottom left and right), 243, 244, 245, 246; E. Richardson, p. 174; The Science Museum, p. 128; Ernest H. Shepard, p. 217; United States Signal Corps, The National Archives, p. 178.

JACKET PHOTOS

Front, clockwise from top: Dreadnought; Queen Victoria; the Prince of Wales; the Bellamys and their servants; the first news of the *Titanic* disaster; Camille Clifford, the original Gibson Girl.

Back, clockwise from top: Albert and Elizabeth, the Duke and Duchess of York; King Edward VII; Queen Mary; London traffic scene; Balmoral portrait; Bank Holiday on Hampstead Heath.

Library of Congress Cataloging in Publication Data

Hardwick, Mollie.
    The world of upstairs, downstairs.
    Includes index.
    1. Upstairs, downstairs.   I. Title.
PN1992.77.U633H3   791.45'7   75-21465
ISBN 0-03-015571-1

First Edition

Book Design by Jos. Trautwein

Printed in the United States of America

10 9 8 7 6 5 4 3 2 1

CONTENTS

PREFACE

No television series has provided more compelling viewing than "Upstairs, Downstairs," which was originated by London Weekend Television and screened in more than thirty countries, from the United Kingdom, where it is set, to the United States, the Antipodes, Eastern Europe, and the Far East.

In its many episodes it has followed the fortunes, misfortunes, and everyday lives of the Bellamy family abovestairs at 165 Eaton Place in London's fashionable Belgravia and those of the other "family" occupying the belowstairs region—their servants. Like the television series, this book chronicles more than three decades, during which time the lives of Richard Bellamy, subsequently Viscount Bellamy of Haversham; his successive wives, Lady Marjorie and Virginia; his son James and ward Georgina have intertwined with the lives of the butler, Mr. Hudson; the cook, Mrs. Bridges; the maids, Rose, Sarah, Daisy, Ruby, and others; and the junior servingmen, Edward, Thomas, Alfred, and Frederick.

The World of Upstairs, Downstairs offers the facts behind the fiction, subordinating the story to its background. In the book, we enter the lives of the Bellamys in 1897, the year of Queen Victoria's Diamond Jubilee, a little more than three years before her death and the accession to the throne of her son, King Edward VII.

In Edward's reign, as in Victoria's, snobbery was rampant and class distinctions acute. It had not always been so. Servants in earlier centuries had often been not hired hands but poor relations of the family. But the gap between servant and master grew wider with time, and in the main the prevailing concept was that expressed by Benjamin Disraeli in his novel *Sybil*:

> *"Our Queen reigns over the greatest nation that ever existed," said Egremont.*
> *"She reigns over two," the young stranger replied. "Two nations, who are as*
> *ignorant of each other's habits, thoughts and feelings as if they were dwellers*
> *in different zones, or inhabitants of different planets; who are formed by a*
> *different breeding, are fed by a different food, are ordered by different*
> *manners, and are not governed by the same laws. Those two nations are the*
> *Rich and the Poor."*

Perhaps the relationships between the two "nations" or "families" of 165 Eaton Place are a trifle idealized. Most employers were, at best, indifferent to and, at worst, callously ready to exploit their servants' dependence on them. A number of times in "Upstairs, Downstairs" we hear a trusted servant being told, after some personal or family misfortune, that provision will be made, security assured. It was by no means frequently so in real life. Used-up servants were discarded into the workhouse as readily as worn-out kitchen utensils were consigned to the dustbin, with never a qualm of conscience.

At the same time, the Bellamys' household is no great liberal establishment. They might have had their servants' welfare at heart, but at any time of the day or night they would not hesitate to press a bell to summon attendance, call for food or drink, or demand an explanation for some discommoding breach of discipline. They aren't employers in the modern sense; they are masters and mistresses. And the servants recognize them as such, ready to do as they are told and to behave themselves in the eyes of their betters, for they know that outside their relatively comfortable "home" there awaits a world of sordidness and even starvation.

The servants, however, have a pride and a hierarchy of their own. Literacy and awareness grow among them as they did among other working people of their time. From the state of blind acceptance in which their predecessors had served they come to question and reason and even argue. The master of the nether regions, Mr. Hudson, by no means enjoys the unchallenged supremacy that would have been his in earlier deacades. A leitmotif of the series is his struggle to maintain the old standards, the status quo, in the changing world about him.

The story of the people of "Upstairs, Downstairs," as presented on television and in the books based on the series, is essentially one of human relationships; yet even these were created, colored, and sometimes destroyed by actual events of the time. *The World of Upstairs, Downstairs* does not retell the stories of the series, which have already been done so well, but rather places characters in the context of the age in which they lived. What I have sought to provide in these pages is the dimension of social history, to fill in the color and the texture of the period from 1897 to 1930—a time of radical change matched only by the period between the end of World War II and the present. Social reform, women's suffrage, European militaristic ferment, all contrast with the lingering rituality of the country-house weekend (with the tactfully adjacent bedrooms for acknowledged "close friends"), the vitality and artificiality of entertainment, the ever-varied vanity of costume and fashion, the elaborate and stylized demands of protocol and behavior—in brief, the pomp and circumstance that both worlds inherited, created, and served.

"Upstairs, Downstairs" on the screen is an entertainment and a passing portrait of an age. With this book I have tried, as we say in television, to "freeze the frame," to fix the flickering image for those who have found its period evocative and wish to linger over its nostalgia.

MOLLIE HARDWICK

The World of Upstairs, Downstairs

12

Queen Victoria in the dress she wore at the Jubilee service

CHAPTER ONE

Sixty Years a Queen

Tuesday, June 22, 1897, was a holiday in the household at 165 Eaton Place, in London's elegant district of Belgravia. The Bellamy family and their servants were not the only ones to leave their home that day, for it was the day of Queen Victoria's Diamond Jubilee, the celebration of her sixty glorious years on the throne of Great Britain, the longest reign in the country's history.

London flowered with loyal greetings: "Our Hearts Thy Throne!" "She Wrought Her People Lasting Good!" As the brillant sunshine of true "Queen's Weather" shone benevolently down, crowds cheered themselves hoarse and waved their hands, sticks, and even their children at the tiny, dumpy figure in the carriage, shaded by a black lace parasol. Tears filled the Queen's faded blue eyes and rolled down her plump cheeks, but they were tears of happiness and pride.

Richard Bellamy, M.P., and his wife, Lady Marjorie, occupied seats in the stand that had cost £25,000 to erect in Constitution Hill. It provided every comfort for the sightseers, including lavatories, ladies' rooms, and telephones; it was a triumph of modern construction. With the Bellamys were their son, James, on holiday from Eton, where he was in his last year before going on to the Royal Military Academy at Sandhurst, and his sister, Elizabeth, the despair of her governess, who was thankful to be free of her, if only for a day.

Somewhere down among the crowds were the servants: Mr. Hudson, the butler, severely and correctly suited in black and wearing his immaculately brushed bowler hat; Mrs. Bridges, the cook, who, like the head parlourmaid Rose and the under-parlourmaid Kate, was in her best holiday finery. Their large picture hats, faithful copies of those worn by ladies of fashion, were laden with artificial flowers and birds; their high-necked summer blouses had huge shoulder-of-mutton sleeves; their long skirts trailed in the summer dust. Even the poor little Irish scullery maid, Emily, wore the best finery she could scrape together, with a feather lent by Rose in her battered hat. Alfred, the footman, had been drinking with Pearce, the coachman, and both were red-faced and unsteady but sober enough to cheer as loudly as the rest. Their straw hats, known as boaters, were tipped back on their heads, and they had loosened their high tight collars. Boisterously, from their precarious place on a wall, they pointed out to each other the celebrities in the procession.

"That's the Princess of Wales in the carriage with 'er. Not 'alf a corker, she ain't—pretty as a picture! Too good for old Tum-Tum, if you ask me."

Preparations in Park Lane for the Jubilee

The Prince of Wales, the future Edward VII, his Danish wife Alexandra, and their children

"Tum-Tum" was the irreverent nickname bestowed on His Royal Highness, Albert Edward, Prince of Wales, whose appetite for food was surpassed only by his appetite for women and whose infidelities to his lovely Danish wife, Alexandra, were as great a source of sorrow to the Queen as his fondness for raffish company. He was a shocking contrast to his sainted father, Albert, the Prince Consort. But, as people said, who could blame him if he played about a bit? He had spent the best years of his life waiting for a throne that he might never occupy, for his mother was seventy-eight now and appeared to be immortal. He was allowed no participation in the serious affairs of state, for the Queen preferred to keep the reins in her own hands. Small wonder if her eldest son had become little more, it seemed, than an elderly playboy. And yet he was popular, a Toff, a Regular Sport, the people said.

Up in the stand, Richard pointed out to Lady Marjorie the imposing figure of Lord Wolseley, Commander-in-Chief, riding in front of the royal carriage, and, at the head of the glittering lines of troops, the giant Captain Ames of the 2nd Life Guards. "The tallest man in the British Army," said James enviously. "I wish I was as tall as that."

His mother patted his hand affectionately. "You're doing very nicely, dear."

James looked longingly at the columns of splendid men on splendid horses. "I'm going to get into the Life Guards, you see if I don't."

His father had caught sight of the patriarchal, bearded Lord Salisbury, the Prime Minister in whose government he served. And there was General Biddulph, the new Black Rod, with his plumed hat, and the lean, bespectacled Arthur Balfour, nephew to the Prime Minister. Richard saw that his wife, too, had seen them—had probably taken note of every member of the government in sight. Lady Marjorie, daughter of that distinguished Tory Lord Southwold, took the keenest interest in all things Parliamentary. It was a pity, Richard thought, that strong-minded ladies like Marjorie were not allowed the privilege of voting, much less of sitting in the House. It would never happen, of course, despite all the work of those respectable campaigners for women's rights. He could foresee the days of the militant suffragettes fast approaching.

The procession wound on towards St. Paul's, where a Thanksgiving Service was to be held at the foot of the steps, for the Queen was too lame to ascend into the cathedral. The heat of the day was lessening as the tired, excited servants wended their way back through the crowds to Eaton Place, chattering of all they had seen.

The evening was to be free for most of them, for the Bellamys were attending a Jubilee dinner. Mrs. Bridges voted that they all "do a show," but there was some difference of opinion as to which it should be. *The Mikado* was still being performed, of course. It always was, though twelve years had passed since it had taken London by storm. Or there was the music hall, in its glorious twilight before the coming of the cinema. At the Pavilion, the Oxford, the Alhambra, the Empire, one could be entertained by stout corseted ladies displaying a great

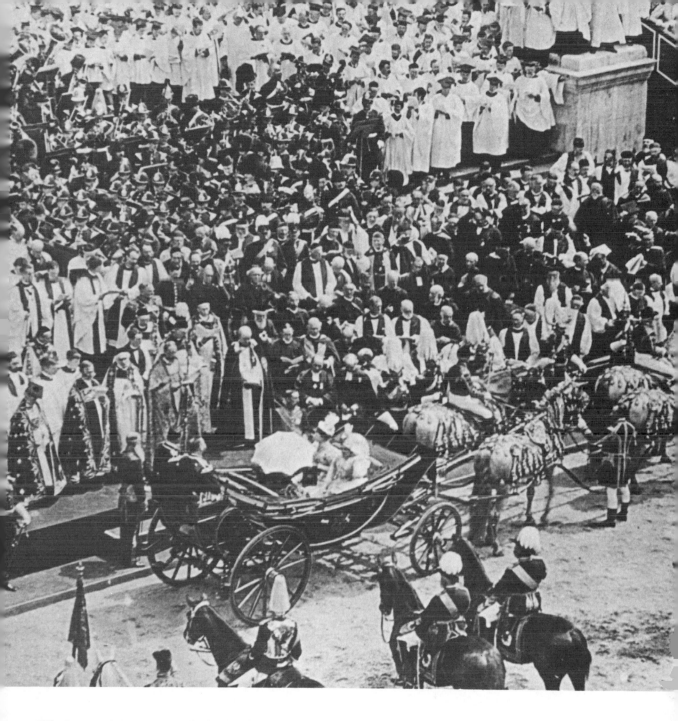

The Queen arriving at St. Paul's for the Thanksgiving Service

deal of glitter and comic men in loud check suits. All the errand boys whistled their songs: Marie Lloyd's saucy "Oh, Mr. Porter," Vesta Victoria's "Our Lodger's Such a Nice Young Man," Florrie Forde's "Waltz Me Around Again, Willie." A young comedian called Charles Chaplin, whose eight-year-old son bore his father's name, was singing ballads about Gay Paree that would never bring him fame or fortune. Those rewards were reserved for his namesake.

18

Theatregoers at a music hall

*The great Marie Lloyd,
much admired by the
Prince of Wales*

American entertainers shared the stage with the home product, Eugene Stratton and R.G. Knowles among them. "Little Tich," the funny man with the top hat and immensely long boots, divided his appearances between England and America; the entertainment world was making a mere lake of the Atlantic.

The English pub—workingmen drinking in a public house

Mrs. Bridges, Rose, and Kate made up their minds to spend the evening at the Empire and with difficulty persuaded Mr. Hudson to accompany them; he would much have preferred a good, serious play. As for Alfred and Mr. Pearce, they went off together to the Crown and Anchor, in nearby Elizabeth Street, a public house that was the traditional meeting place for the local butlers, footmen, valets, and coachmen. The classes were as sharply divided in their drinking habits as in everything else; no "gentleman" would have dreamed of frequenting the Crown and Anchor, any more than his servant would have ventured into the Ritz or the Savoy, even if he had had money in his pocket.

There was no familiarity between servants and masters in the Bellamy household, but there was mutual respect and even affection. Miss Elizabeth was Rose's particular pet, and Mrs. Bridges had a soft spot for Master James, whose tuck-boxes were filled at the start of every school term with her excellent cakes. Richard Bellamy trusted Mr. Hudson implicitly; Lady Marjorie depended greatly on her elderly personal maid, Miss Roberts. Mrs. Bridges might shout and scold at the younger maids, but cruelty to them was unknown, and their working and living conditions were reasonable, if not luxurious. *Punch* had published an illustrated joke showing a lady giving a visitor a tour of the house. Pausing at the door of a dark cellar whose walls streamed with damp, the visitor commented on its unhealthy appearance. "Oh, it's all right—nobody sleeps in here but the kitchen maid," replied his hostess. This was a far cry from the Bellamy household, needless to say.

The work was hard, of course, and Jubilee days came round very seldom. Richard Bellamy's position as a Member of Parliament demanded that frequent dinner parties be given, and though No. 165 was smaller than many of its neighbours, the handsome dining table, with its expanding wings, could seat a fair number. The enormous meals, of eight or nine courses, occupied the entire staff, with Mrs. Bridges cooking, Mr. Hudson, Alfred, and Rose doing the serving, and Emily in the kitchen dealing with the mountains of used plates and dishes. Although an electric dishwasher had been invented by an American woman in 1889, the Bellamys' kitchen was not sufficiently modern to include such a device.

An eloquent insight into servant life

From a film taken at Balmoral in 1896: Czar Nicholas is on the Queen's right and the Czarina stands directly behind the carriage.

But the summer dusk of that Jubilee evening was lit by a brilliant intermingling of thousands of tiny gas jets with electric light bulbs. The effect was spectacular, particularly to those among the crowds whose youth had known nothing brighter than candles and oil lamps. "What scientific miracles we live among!" they exclaimed. Only a year before Guglielmo Marconi had demonstrated on Salisbury Plain a magic unknown to its long-vanished Druids: the possibility of wireless telegraphy.

There were many other signs of inventive genius. Air-conditioning had begun, though in a primitive form. The telephone (an instrument regarded by Mr. Hudson with distrustful disapproval) was coming more and more into use as a means of communication. That year, 1897, the first experimental automatic switchboard, incorporating 200 lines, was installed at Winchester House in London's Old Broad Street. Even the Queen's household used the telephone. Her Majesty had condescended to converse through one as long ago as 1878. She was, of course, extremely progressive for such an elderly lady. At Balmoral, in '96, she had graciously permitted herself and some of the royal family to be "photographed by the new cinematograph process," thus becoming the first monarch to be filmed. Among the children jumping about on the grass for the photographer's benefit was a two-year-old boy who would in turn become Prince of Wales, King Edward VIII, and the virtually exiled Duke of Windsor; and two of the house guests at Balmoral, who were photographed planting a tree, were "Nicky and Alicky," the Emperor Nicholas II and the Empress Alexandra Feodorovna of Russia, destined for a terrible death twenty-two years later.

As for the motorcar, that other dangerous innovation, it was catching on, in defiance of all those who had said it could not possibly be roadworthy. The Arnold, the first petrol-driven car known definitely to have been manufactured for sale in England, had made its first extended road trial from East Peckham to Bromley, Kent, in November 1896. *Punch* speculated on the plight of a fox hunter contemplating with dismay a placard advertising "THE MOTOR HUNT. Only automatic foxes used. No cruelty, no blank days. Electric and steam horses for hire at the meets."

Mr. Pearce laughed like everybody else. The very idea that his stables could be occupied by one of those stinking, clumsy, noisy monsters! He would, he told Alfred, still be driving 'osses in another twenty years and more, maybe. But Lady Marjoric, whose handsome eyes missed nothing in the way of fashionable and convenient novelties, was fascinated by the photographs of the auto car they

Traffic jam in the city

Front covers of typical "Penny Dreadfuls"

had called "Adam." When the thing was more advanced and more dignified in appearance, she would certainly ask Richard to order one.

The Bellamys were not great readers. *The Times,* the *Illustrated London News,* and of course *Punch* were read in the morning room, but little else. Richard, for a Tory politician, was a liberal-minded man, but he had no time for such radical-minded works as the novels of young H.G. Wells, who, he thought, was really carrying this modern craze for science too far in such fantasies as *The Time Machine* and *The Invisible Man,* which he had glanced at and put down again. Nor would he waste his time on rough stuff like the Polish Joseph Conrad's sea yarns *The Nigger of the Narcissus* and *An Outcast of the Islands.* W.W. Jacobs' short stories about comic sailormen were a different matter—something light to pick up when he was tired out after a long day in the House. The newly published poems by A.E. Housman, *A Shropshire Lad*, were of no interest to him, nor the dark, brooding novels of Thomas Hardy.

As for Lady Marjorie, she had ordered one or two novels by the best-selling lady author, Marie Corelli, but after a glance at *The Sorrows of Satan* and *The Mighty Atom* she had thrown the books aside as "romantic rubbish only fit for housemaids." Rose, who liked a nice read, had picked one up, asked permission to borrow it, and had been entranced by Miss Corelli's purple passages and high-flown sentiments. As for Mrs. Bridges, she was content with *Hilda's Home Companion* and Mr. Hudson's daily reading aloud from the newspaper.

Lady Marjorie played the piano brilliantly. She enjoyed concerts at the Albert Hall and the Queen's Hall, particularly when the programme featured some modern work like the *Indian Suite* by the American composer Edward Mac-Dowell or the very new and amusing symphonic poem by Paul Dukas, *The Sorcerer's Apprentice*. Opera, too, she liked. Richard did not care greatly for it, so she usually attended the Royal Opera House, Covent Garden, with her widowed friend Lady Prudence Fairfax. There, in a box, the two stately ladies in their low-cut gowns, feathers, and jewels would listen entranced to the melodies of Verdi and of Puccini, whose *La Bohème* had been the sensation of the operatic world the previous year.

As to plays, she preferred them light and entertaining. The "naturalistic" dramas of Henrik Ibsen were far too doom-laden for her and so full of symbolism and boring things of that kind. *Ghosts* had been positively nasty, she thought, though she was not easily shocked and had been less horrified than annoyed when the Oscar Wilde scandal had broken in 1895.

"Ridiculous man! Why couldn't he have kept his idiotic private life to himself, and then we could have had more delicious things like *The Importance of Being Earnest?* Instead of which he's in prison, and we have to put up with this tiresome George Bernard Shaw and his intelligent females who talk *all* the time and do something quite unexpected at the end of the play, like *Candida*. Ah well, we shall be visiting Paris in the autumn, and then we can see some ballet—one hardly ever sees it here."

Neither Lady Marjorie nor Richard approved of the Fabian Society, a Socialist movement whose leading lights were Sidney and Beatrice Webb, writers and historians, the critic and playwright George Bernard Shaw, and the remarkable Annie Besant, whose many-sided career had brought her what some called fame and others notoriety, including as it did propagandist work for birth control, political agitation, and advocacy for the doctrine of freethinking. Certainly, the Fabians opposed the revolutionary Socialism of the period, based on the doctrines of Karl Marx, but Richard, though he had been known to sympathize with the Liberal Opposition on some questions, feared that the new movement might well lead to the formation of a third political party that could only divide and weaken the two great traditional ones, Tory and Liberal. He was right, of course. In less than three years the Socialists and trade-union delegates had met to found the Labour Representation Committee. By 1906 it would be calling itself the Labour Party.

The staff were not sympathetic to the Fabians either. Their political attitudes (if they could be said to have any) were dictated by Mr. Hudson, the arbiter of all matters Downstairs. Conservative by nature, utterly loyal to his Tory masters, he held that there could be no workable alternative to the class system. Revolution was utterly foreign to his character. As for the rest of the staff, all came from working-class homes and knew the horrors of poverty that might await them in the cruel world outside the safety and warmth of No. 165. It was not for them to make protests and demand rights. Hard-worked and poorly paid they might be, but they had a roof over their heads and three meals a day. It was a great deal in 1897.

The Bellamys, although they observed the Christian festivals and went to church with fair regularity, were not essentially religious as a family. Piety was not a notable characteristic of the rich and fashionable of Belgravia. They did not, therefore, stipulate any particular devotional requirement when they engaged a servant, unlike those families who advertised for a cook and house-parlourmaid: "Early risers. Churchwomen." When they attended church, it was St. Paul's, Knightsbridge. Mr. Hudson presented himself every Sunday at Belgrave Presbyterian Church, Halkin Street West; Rose and Kate attended Early Service at St. Peter's, Eaton Square, because it fitted in with their duties better than the service of Matins; and Irish Emily tramped in her shabby boots to the Oratory, South Kensington. Pearce was not known to frequent any place of worship, but Alfred attended some strange chapel, one of the new denominations that were filtering over from America. He was something of a religious maniac, more than a little unbalanced. Mr. Hudson had no time for these wild sects with their (to him) ungodly goings-on and prophecies of doom. In this he was at one with the Queen, a vigorous opponent of all who seemed to her to be undermining the Anglican Church.

The Jubilee celebration was over, but "Queen's Weather" still prevailed in London for the garden party at Buckingham Palace that Richard and Lady Marjorie attended on June 28. Adventurous motorists were tempted out onto the roads, rushing along in clouds of dust at the dangerous maximum speed of 14 miles per hour. In September, a nine-year-old boy was killed in Hackney by a motor-taxi belonging to the Electric Cab Company. It was his own fault, for he had been stealing a ride on one of the cab's springs when his coat became

"Say what ye will, he was a Grand Old Man."

entangled in the chain-drive; but Mrs. Bridges gloomily announced that before they knew where they were the streets of London would be choked with the bleeding corpses of innocent pedestrians. She was particularly indignant to hear from Mr. Hudson that a woman had actually dared to take the wheel—the actress Minnie Palmer, who had bought a car from the Daimler Company and was driving it around Scotland. "But then what can you expect, actresses? Up to everything, they are."

"Come now, Mrs. Bridges," Mr. Hudson remonstrated. "I am sure Miss Ellen Terry would never be so unwomanly as to lend herself to such a thing— nor would Miss Marie Tempest. Though," he added thoughtfully, "I am not so sure about Mademoiselle Sarah Bernhardt. These foreigners are not like ourselves."

The turn of the year came. In May 1898 the country heard with sadness of the death of the great Liberal statesman William Ewart Gladstone. He was eighty-

England vs. Australia at the Oval

nine. When he was born, in 1809, the Battle of Trafalgar was still fresh in people's memories, and the Battle of Waterloo would not be fought for another six years. He had become Leader of the Liberal Party in 1867, had four times been Prime Minister, had crossed swords in the House with that other political giant, Disraeli, and had incurred the steady disapproval of his Queen. "I did not like the man," she said when told of his death. "How can I say I am sorry when I am not?"

In the Bellamy household the news was received more charitably.

"Whatever you say, Marjorie," said Richard, laying down *The Times,* "Mr. Gladstone was the greatest reformer of our era. I won't say that I haven't criticized him strongly over some of his measures. He was 'the People's William' and as such they'll remember him with gratitude."

"I was not going to say anything," his wife answered, "except that I quite agreed with Father when he said that Mr. Gladstone's views on Ireland were utterly crass. I hope that we shall hear no more now about this ridiculous Home Rule policy."

Downstairs, Mr. Hudson was entering Mr. Gladstone's death on the flyleaf of his Bible, where he recorded notable events. "A Grand Old Man," he pronounced. "Say what ye will, he was a Grand Old Man."

The summer of 1898 was pleasant, on the face of it. *The Belle of New York* had come to the Adelphi Theatre and was delighting London with its catchy tunes and amusing plot. Mr. Hudson made frequent weekend excursions to Lord's Cricket Ground and the Oval, Kensington, to see such giants as Kumar Shri Ranjit Sinhji, "the Black Prince of Cricket," and W.G. Grace, the lavishly bearded "demon doctor." The artistic Londoner was admiring the paintings of

"Trouble"—Victorian married life as portrayed by the popular painter W. Q. Orchardson

Mr. William Quiller Orchardson, with their Regency-costumed Victorians playing cards and instruments with equal picturesqueness and their contemporary scenes of fashionably dressed couples (the gentleman in white tie and tails, the lady in bare-shouldered evening dress and Grecian-styled hair) enduring the trials of marital break-up. "The First Cloud" and "Trouble" showed two such painful incidents, while "Her Mother's Voice" portrayed an aristocratic gentleman listening broodily in his drawing room to the warblings of his teenage daughter at the piano. With the immense steps taken forward in photography, the late Victorians liked their pictures realistic and exciting.

Athletic young ladies in gigot-sleeved outdoor suits and "Robin Hood" feathered hats scurried about the country lanes on bicycles. No one at 165 Eaton Place had a bicycle, for though accepted in the country, these vehicles were

Nanny in charge in Kensington Gardens

Two fashionably overdressed young ladies

looked down on in town as being suitable only for errand boys. Children in London were allowed no such dangerous toys. Heavily overdressed in clothes the replica of their parents', small boys in knickerbocker or sailor suits, small girls in enveloping dresses with long sleeves, bonnets, and woollen stockings, they played sedately in Kensington Gardens, while their infant brothers and sisters, equally overdressed, were pushed around Hyde Park in dignified perambulators attended by high-capped, starch-collared nannies. Mrs. Bridges took a painful pleasure in peering, during her afternoons off, into these perambulators, at their well-fed beribboned contents. Her title of "Mrs." was purely honorary. In fact, all cooks were addressed as married women, a gesture of courtesy towards their important status in the household. Kate Bridges was single, several times "disappointed" in likely suitors, and deeply fond of children. Master James was

A tradition of the English summer: Henley Regatta

a dear boy, even though spoilt by his mother, but only a substitute for the sons she might herself have had.

The Bellamys went to Henley Regatta in July, enjoying, as usual, the parade of many-coloured summer dresses and smart boating gear and leaving before the Cockney holiday-makers invaded the river with their twanging banjos and loud-laughing young women. There were motorcars everywhere; even from the train they were to be seen chugging their way along the roads to Henley. Really, said Lady Marjorie, the world was shrinking rapidly. A Captain Joshua Slocum was reported to have sailed round the world in his tiny oyster boat, *Spray,* landing after his thirty-eight-month voyage at Fairhaven, Massachusetts. Motor-coach tours were actually being organized, between London and Clacton-on-Sea in Essex, taking five and one half hours each way to cover the seventy miles. Lady Marjorie supposed the staff would be using such a service for their annual summer outing next year.

August 12 came, the beginning of the game season, and they were off to Scotland for the shooting. Rose accompanied Lady Marjorie as maid. Alfred came as valet to Richard, who would have preferred someone more polished and reliable. The rest of the staff stayed at Eaton Place, enjoying some leisure and thankful not to be on "board wages"—in other words, receiving only their keep, without money, as was the case in so many London houses. London was a dead place without its nobility and gentry; only tourists and native Cockneys were to be seen in the streets and parks. The Queen was in Scotland, the Prince of Wales at his country home, Sandringham, in Norfolk, bringing down unlucky birds by the score and entertaining his last and most influential mistress, the Honourable Mrs. George Keppel. People with time on their hands (James Bellamy, on leave from Sandhurst, included) were devouring Anthony Hope's romantic adventure novel, *Rupert of Hentzau,* sequel to the stirring *The Prisoner of Zenda,* which had come out four years earlier. It all seemed like a normal English summer.

Yet a certain optical specialist, Dr. Arthur Conan Doyle, observed that "the shadow of South Africa was falling upon England, and before it passed my personal fortunes, as well as so many more, were destined to be involved in it." He was right. Author of the wildly successful Sherlock Holmes stories and of several distinguished historical novels, he was also a man of action. In 1896, when trouble broke out on the border of Egypt, "the storm centre of the world," as he called it, he happened to be there on holiday with his delicate wife. When

Arthur Conan D

the South African war broke out in 1899 he would be there also, doctoring to the fever-stricken troops. Now, in September 1898, he heard in his Surrey home of the struggle in the Sudan and the defeat by Kitchener of the Mahdi, a religious leader who claimed to be the Messiah, and his followers, the dervishes. It seemed well; so thought the Queen. Britain was raising her flag again in the country where her hero, General Gordon, had been savagely murdered by the dervishes at the siege of Khartoum in 1885. Dr. Conan Doyle lit his pipe contentedly but noted with concern that there were troubles in China that might have serious consequences in the future.

36

Downstairs teatime

The average Englishman was not concerned with China. Intellectuals were more interested in the poignant *Ballad of Reading Gaol,* written by the disgraced Oscar Wilde in his imprisonment, and in the sensational C-sharp minor prelude by the Russian composer Sergei Rachmaninoff. They shivered agreeably at Henry James's ghost story, *The Turn of the Screw,* and a few months later young men of James Bellamy's age chortled over Rudyard Kipling's *Stalky and Co.,* for their own schooldays were fresh in their memories. At the Court Theatre the Bellamys were charmed by *Trelawny of the Wells,* a comedy about earlier Victorian actors by Sir Arthur Wing Pinero.

Another year of what seemed to be progress had passed before headlines were to startle the man in the street: There was war between the Boers and the British in South Africa.

It was October 11, 1899. There had been no major warfare involving Britain since the Crimean War, in mid-century, now forgotten by all but the elderly. Mrs. Bridges's father had died a frustrated man, longing to go soldiering but with no opportunity. Kate's grandfather had died at Sebastopol, but she had no idea where it was. Rose remembered her parents talking about a visit made by Lord Lucan to Southwold, long, long ago; and most of them had heard of "The Charge of the Light Brigade," Lord Tennyson's stirring poem. But this war, which had been brewing since the ill-advised Jameson raid in 1895, was to involve something like a quarter of a million British soldiers in the fight against President Kruger of the Transvaal and the other Boer republic in South Africa, the Orange Free State.

It began disastrously. Between December 10 and 17 three battles had been lost by British generals, at Stormberg, Magersfontein, and Colenso. During that Black Week Mr. Hudson shook his head many times over the newspapers, and reinforcements were despatched to South Africa whistling and singing the music-hall ballad "Goodbye Dolly Gray," which was to be associated for all time with the Boer War, though it had, in fact, started life as a song of the Spanish-American conflict of 1898. Rose and Kate, shopping for the household, watched with admiration the khaki-clad men marching to Victoria Station.

"Red coats they'd have had in my pa's time," said Mrs. Bridges. "Very smart they looked, but it made 'em easy targets, poor lads. Maybe this lot'll be luckier."

She was, unfortunately, wrong. The year 1900 came in with news of terrible casualties in the besieged towns of Mafcking, Kimberley, and Ladysmith.

Currency used in the Siege of Mafeking. The figures represent a Boer and a Briton and are taken from drawings by Colonel Baden-Powell.

Boers manning their trenches outside Mafeking

CHAPTER TWO

The End of an Era

People were calling it the twentieth century, though in fact that would not begin until the next New Year. Normally it would have been a time of pleasurable excitement, but the first two months of the year were darkened by grave news from South Africa. Not since the days of the Indian Mutiny had there been such fearful sieges. In Ladysmith, battered by the Boers, the beleaguered garrisons and over twenty thousand inhabitants were threatened by starvation, and a terrible outbreak of enteric fever accounted for more lives than the Boers' Mauser bullets. Londoners went about in gloom as the news grew worse.

Then, at the end of February, the martyrdom of Ladysmith ended, and the tide of war began to flow against the Boers, as Lord Roberts, Lord Kitchener, and Sir Redvers Buller headed triumphant attacks. The town of Mafeking was relieved in May, and President Kruger took flight. The war would continue sporadically for two more years, but the worst of the fighting was over.

Richard Bellamy, tired but relieved after a long sitting at the House, brought the good news home to Marjorie. He was jubilant that Colonial Secretary "Joe" Chamberlain's conduct of the war was finally justified. His attitudes had drawn censure upon him from many, particularly from British Radicals, who had attributed all kinds of strange motives to his giant struggle with Kruger, including the unlikely one of "feathering his own nest."

"If this world of ours ever achieves lasting peace," said Richard, "we shall have Chamberlain and men like him to thank for it."

SOCIAL LIFE IN THE ARMY.

ILLUSTRATIONS BY G.M. PAYNE.

100 UP.

UNDER CANVAS.
A CANTEEN CONCERT.

AT THE SERGEANTS BALL.

AT THE REGIMENTAL SPORTS.

ON THE STRENGTH.

CHURCH PARADE.

A SOLDIER'S WEDDING IN INDIA.

But Chamberlain was not the only target for blame. As the Boer War drew to its close, rumours came back to England of fearful brutalities committed by British soldiers on their enemies. Mr. Hudson, glancing over *The Times*'s foreign correspondence section before it went upstairs, was horrified. Insular by nature, he was always ready to believe anything bad about foreigners, but none of their misdeeds had ever shocked him so much as this campaign of vile accusations against us, the British. With flushed face and glittering spectacles, he read out a selection of the details to Mrs. Bridges.

"Well, I never!" exclaimed that lady, pausing in her refilling of the teapot. "Why, who'd say nasty things like that?"

"The Dutch, Mrs. Bridges. And the Germans. It says here that there have been indignation meetings all over Europe protesting against these—these alleged atrocities. Even clergymen have been banding together to defame our brave boys."

He had not noticed Kate, on her way back from the kitchen, looking over his shoulder. "Ooh!" she squeaked. "It says they eat babies! They never, do they, Mr. Hudson? I mean, people don't, only tigers and such."

Mr. Hudson quelled her with a look. "Of course not. And kindly keep your eyes to yourself, Kate. There are details here not fit for female reading."

Mrs. Bridges, who had been tut-tutting over the paper herself, said indignantly, "I don't believe a word of it. Tommy Atkins isn't a brute like them Boers." (Tommy Atkins was the name given by the Duke of Wellington at random, remembering a gallant casualty of the Peninsular Wars, to the "specimen" soldier of War Department documents.)

It was the opinion of all Britain. That vehement author, Rudyard Kipling, had brought home the trials and humours of the soldier to his readers in *Barrack-Room Ballads*, catchy, colloquial, outspoken verses that shook up a people who had never given much thought to the British soldier. In the past he had been an adventurer, a mercenary going to war for what he could get, then a "lobster," red-coated and equally scarlet of reputation, thrown out of pubs more or less on sight and generally despised. Now Kipling had made a rueful folk hero of "Thomas Atkins." Lady Marjorie and many of her kind declared Kipling's down-to-earth ballads "coarse," but they were uttered by the voice of a prophet whose Anglo-Indian background gave him a unique understanding of the fighting man serving abroad and whose piercing eyes saw through the tumult

The pleasant side of military life—rarely enjoyed by the ordinary soldier

and the shouting and the "pomp of yesterday," which had, until his day, meant war to the British nation.

A new phenomenon had come to Britain, nourished by the stresses of the Boer War. In a house in Bloomsbury a young girl called Clemence Dumas, who would one day be known at 165 Eaton Place as Sarah, was acting as assistant to a spiritualist medium. In the late 1840s the Fox sisters, of Hydesville near Rochester, New York, had become the first known "mediums" between the spirit world and the world of concrete reality. Since their time the movement had acquired a name, spread across the Atlantic, and been taken up by such distinguished men as the physicist and chemist Sir William Crookes. In 1882 the Society for Psychical Research had been founded, and other study centres had been set up in France, Germany, Italy, and the United States. Dr. Arthur Conan Doyle, that ardent campaigner for the reputation of Tommy Atkins, had, in addition to his other pursuits, cautiously taken up the cause of spiritualism. There had been many exposures of fraudulent mediums, and even the most genuine of them were subject to the Vagrancy Act of 1824, under which they might be imprisoned for fortunetelling. Clemence and her employer, Miss Pagenell, undertook the comforting of the anxious or bereaved relatives of soldiers at the risk of their freedom.

But in London ordinary life went on. Society talked in sanctimonious whispers of the death of Oscar Wilde in Paris, his brilliant, thrown-away life ended in disgrace. James, in the summer, was thrilled to see one of the earliest moving pictures showing the fighting at Kimberley. It seemed incredible, the dark, jerkily moving forms that had been real men, fighting and dying in a landscape utterly foreign to James. He wondered if he would find himself, some day, in some such unreal setting, a soldier amid soldiers, and if others, sitting in biograph theatres, would see him as he saw the heroes of Kimberley. It was less disturbing to read H. G. Wells's new flight of science-fiction fancy, *The First Men in the Moon* (as if men could ever dream of reaching it!), or to go with the family to a comedy scarcely more fantastic, F. Anstey's play *The Brass Bottle* at the Strand Theatre. It was about a young architect who came into possession of a brass bottle from the East that, unknown to him, contained a genie of great power and monumental stupidity. James's mind did not run to this sort of fantasy; he laughed when his friends did, thinking it agreeable nonsense.

In the summer of 1900 Lady Marjorie's patience with her daughter Elizabeth finally snapped. Governess after governess had departed, in tears or tantrums,

A Victorian photograph of the "spirit world"

Count von Zeppelin's giant airship

after being subjected to Elizabeth's wilfulness and disobedience. Reluctantly, Richard, whose favourite she was, agreed that if Elizabeth were to get any sort of disciplined education at all she must go away to school—finishing school, of course. They settled on the highly recommended establishment of Frau Beck at Dresden. German discipline was known to be excellent, and the Continental friendships Elizabeth would make might be very useful to her in the future.

Mr. Hudson, when he heard the news, looked gloomy. To him Germany was a name of doom. Neglecting no item in the newspapers, he had read that Admiral von Tirpitz, Secretary of State for the Imperial German Navy, had persuaded the Reichstag to pass an act that in a few years was bound to double the navy's strength. He had read, too, of the construction of a cigar-shaped dirigible airship by Count Ferdinand von Zeppelin. "It bodes no good," he said to Mrs. Bridges. "Conspiracy and faction, if you ask me."

"Oh, go on!" She waved a knitting needle at him. "Gunpowder, treason, and plot, you'll be saying next. Why, that there Kaiser's the Queen's own grandson,

Princess Vicky of Prussia's eldest. He wouldn't do nothing to harm his own grandma's country."

Mr. Hudson said nothing but continued polishing the silver.

In the drawing room, Lady Prudence Fairfax was looking critically about her. "All very nice, Marjorie dear. But just a teeny bit old-fashioned, don't you

"Mr. Hudson said nothing but continued polishing the silver."

think? I mean, portraits of rather stuffy-looking people and all those heavy gilt frames. Oh, I'm sure they're all Southwolds and by Romney and Reynolds and people like that, but . . . well, really." She flourished a large magazine in an elegant green cover. "There's the sweetest thing in this month's *Studio*. I thought of commissioning him to paint one for me."

Lady Marjorie looked at the illustration quizzically. "What is it? Looks like a nightmare to me."

"Oh, I don't know what it's meant to be. That hardly matters, does it? Look at the curves, that marvellous line. . . . Yes, I do think I shall have to have it. And I've seen the most delicious furniture at Liberty's, all hand-made and so stark and simple. I think I'll get rid of that old-fashioned mahogany poor Arthur was so fond of. One must change with the times, and this *is* the twentieth century."

Lady Marjorie looked around at her heirlooms. "Not quite. Not yet."

With a last lingering look at the painting by Claude Monet, Lady Prudence closed the *Studio*. She would in time store up considerable comfort for her old age by collecting small paintings that took her fancy by the Impressionists Renoir, Pissarro, Degas, artists dismissed by many of her contemporaries as crude, gaudy, and violent. The sort of pictures that appealed to the majority were the highly realistic works of G. H. Boughton, an Englishman taken to America in infancy and brought up in Albany, New York. On many a wall hung reproductions of his scenes of Dutch life, or his idyllic portrayal of the young William Shakespeare strolling with Anne Hathaway by the Avon.

Of all the Bellamys' circle only Lady Prudence took the trouble to get hold of a volume of Havelock Ellis' *Studies in the Psychology of Sex*. When it first appeared in the year of the Jubilee, the journal of the British Medical Association refused to review it, warning, "It is especially important that such matters should not be discussed by the man in the street." Lady Prudence found Ellis quite astonishing, but the book could hardly be a conversational gambit at even the most sophisticated dinner parties.

The two ladies made a charming, formal picture as they sat, very upright, drinking tea poured from the elaborate Georgian silver teapot that had been among Lady Marjorie's wedding presents from her parents. The cups and saucers were of delicate flowered porcelain, the sandwiches cut wafer-thin by Mrs. Bridges. The ladies' clothes were expensive, flowing, heavily trimmed, fastened with dozens of tiny buttons and hooks-and-eyes that would be dealt with at dressing times and bedtime by the fingers of their personal maids, and their ample figures were crammed into stiff whalebone corsets that gave them the appearance of having swanlike busts and small waists. Round the hem of Lady Prudence's walking-costume skirt was sewn a length of brush-braid, to catch the mud and grime of the pavement as she made the short journey from door to carriage. When her garments were in need of cleaning, it would be done by hand—again by her maid—with petrol, which left the garment smelling so unpleasant that it would be put in the garden on a clothesline until the odour had faded somewhat. Otherwise the maid might use a mixture of fuller's earth, ammonia, and benzine, almost equally as pungent. Any material that was unwashable, such as white silk, would be cleaned with stale bread crumbs.

The ritual of afternoon tea

Ladies' maids, though envied by the rest of the staff as being highly privileged, worked hard for their living.

Although she was taking tea with a close friend, Lady Prudence retained her hat and gloves. This was one of the endless commandments of Victorian etiquette, ruling everything from the leaving of a visiting card to the conduct of a grand dinner party. Lady Prudence might remove her gloves if asked to partake of bread and butter, for the butter would make them greasy; but for the consumption of sandwiches and biscuits she would retain them. Lady Marjorie, when pouring the tea, would not have dreamed of putting the milk in the cups first; only the "socially impossible" did that and were known derisively as "miffers" milk-in-firsts. Richard Bellamy, calling on a lady, would take his hat and stick into the drawing room with him, as every gentleman must, to signify delicately that his visit was not sufficiently intimate to warrant leaving them in the hall. The length of his visit, like that of everyone else in society, was controlled by strict formalities. Even if one's hostess were to ask, "Can you not stay a little longer?" the enquiry would be taken, as it was meant, as a mere social cliché.

The world of Upstairs, Downstairs was ruled by these things. Outside there were, of course, changes, relaxations that were strongly disapproved of by such diehards as old Lady Southwold, Lady Marjorie's mother. But in the household of the Bellamys things went on as they always had done and always would do, it seemed.

But a time was coming when nothing would be quite the same, for the longest reign in English history was moving to its close.

Ever since the outbreak of the Boer War things had been worsening in the personal life of Queen Victoria. She had lost a son-in-law, Prince Henry of Battenburg, not long before, and in 1900 her son Prince Alfred, "Affie," died suddenly. Her eyesight was weakening, for she had double cataracts that threatened to make her blind. Another loss came with the death of her grandson, Prince Christian Victor of Schleswig-Holstein; and her beloved eldest daughter, "Vicky," the Empress Frederick of Prussia, was dangerously ill. With these troubles, and the anxiety of South Africa and the Boxer Rebellion in China, she was finding it difficult to sleep. "It is hard at eighty-one!" she exclaimed in a moment of self-pity.

The winter of 1900–1901 was bitter; the twentieth century proper came in with storms. The Queen was unwell, struggling against illness, age, and the

The genuine whalebone corset

The royal yacht Alberta *off Cowes, Isle of Wight*

darkening of her sight. On January 13, 1901, she closed the journal she had kept all her life and two days later took to her bed. On January 22 a bulletin was issued by her medical attendants: "The Queen is slowly sinking."

She died at Osborne, the house on the Isle of Wight in which she and Albert had taken such pride. One of the royal yachts, *Alberta*, brought her coffin to the mainland, and a special train took it to Victoria Station. The Bellamys and their servants were among the thousands who watched, awestruck, in streets decked with purple cashmere trimmed with white satin bows, as the Queen made her last journey to Paddington, on her way to Windsor. The coffin was very small (the Queen had been less than five feet tall) and travelled on a gun carriage, partially draped with the red, white, and blue of the Royal Standard and topped with the crown. Bands played funeral music, including laments for dead chieftains of the Highlands she had loved so much. Even the hardest-hearted among the crowds wept for the woman who had ruled over them for sixty-four years, and thought of the glorious day, only four years earlier, when they had cheered her Jubilee.

But Mr. Hudson, though a tear moistened his eye, was keeping a sharp watch on the Queen's grandson, Kaiser Wilhelm of Prussia, who had been at her

The Queen's funeral procession, led by Edward VII and the Kaiser Wilhelm, arrives at Paddington.

deathbed and who rode beside her other descendants in the funeral procession. He had the unmistakable air of a man who thinks he has the right to take the centre of the stage on all occasions. He bore himself stiffly, consciously on parade. His tomcat moustachios bristled. The white plumes on his hat seemed to be trying to outdazzle those of his companions, the new King Edward VII and the Duke of Connaught. The withered arm, which had contributed to his lifelong arrogance, was hidden beneath his cloak.

It was said that the Kaiser had been untiring in his vigil by the late Queen's deathbed and had even tried to lift her into her coffin, a privilege that he was denied by two of his cousins. Certainly, he *was* the Queen's grandson, child of her eldest daughter; but need he be quite so prominent in this funeral scene? Mr. Hudson, who did not make any distinction between Boers and Germans, distrusted the Kaiser strongly. He also distrusted the new King, the sixty-year-old monarch who had had to wait so many years for his throne and had passed them travelling abroad, keeping a string of racehorses and mistresses, gambling and playing about in a most unseemly fashion, thought Mr. Hudson. What kind of a king would he make?

"A very good one, I'd be prepared to wager," said Richard Bellamy to his wife. "The Queen was popular, but it was in spite of her faults, not because of her virtues. She was an autocrat, an eccentric, and she never understood party politics. She kept herself shut up at Windsor when her people wanted to see her among them."

"Crowds gave her a headache," said Lady Marjorie.

"Crowned heads must expect to have headaches. Now the King is very different. When he met the Privy Council the day after his mother's death, he made a remarkable speech without using a single note, and I was told he consulted nobody as to what he should say. 'I am fully determined to be a constitutional monarch in the strictest sense of the word,' he told the Council. And I believe he will be."

Richard was proved right. King Edward's reign of only nine years was to be far more cheerful for his country than his mother's had been. He enjoyed power and he enjoyed pleasure. He had Buckingham Palace redecorated (Victoria had never liked it) and established his court there instead of at Windsor, to the delight of Londoners. His beautiful wife and their family were the darlings of the public. In times to come people would talk of the Edwardian Golden Age, now just beginning.

Edward VII's sitting room in Buckingham Palace

McKinley's Inauguration, 1901, shortly before his assassination

CHAPTER THREE

The Edwardian Spring

The year 1901 saw another death, and another accession, far away across the Atlantic. On September 6 President McKinley was shot by an anarchist, and on September 14, the day of his death, Theodore Roosevelt took the oath as twenty-sixth President of the United States. A man of many parts, he had become a national hero when, in the Spanish-American War of 1898, he had personally led the charge of the Rough Riders in the battle of San Juan Hill. Soon afterwards, as Governor of New York, he showed himself to be a notable reformer and enemy of corruption of all kinds. It was said of him that as President "he entered men's lives, kindled fires in them, impelled them to scorn ease and safety and rejoice to do the fine, the difficult thing." As unlike as possible the crowned ruler of Great Britain whose nickname of "Teddy" he shared, he was as powerful an influence on his country and his times.

Five years after he became President he was to be awarded the Nobel Peace Prize for his mediation after the Russo-Japanese War. The prizes were first distributed in 1901, on the anniversary of the death of Alfred Bernhard Nobel, the Swedish chemist and engineer who, somewhat ironically, had amassed a great fortune from his discovery and manufacture of dynamite and other explosives. William Roentgen, recipient of the 1901 Nobel Physics Prize, had discovered a mysterious new radiation—X rays, as they were soon called. They would revolutionize the diagnosis and treatment of disease.

In this year of change and surprises it was not, perhaps, strange that a wildly popular and much-mourned figure should rise from the dead, to the joy of the reading public. In August 1901 Sherlock Holmes, last heard of locked in a death embrace with the arch-villain Moriarty on the brink of the terrible Reichenbach Falls, came back to the scene in Conan Doyle's most thrilling long story, *The Hound of the Baskervilles*. After the first instalment had appeared in the *Strand* magazine, eager queues at the bookstalls awaited further news of the great detective, his faithful henchman Dr. Watson, and the phantom hound whose appearance on Dartmoor was enough to frighten people to death.

Another exciting work appeared, this time from the pen of Kipling: the novel *Kim*, telling the story of Kimball O'Hara, an orphan boy travelling through India with a wise old Tibetan lama and learning enough of that mysterious country to be of use to the British Secret Service. Nothing quite like *Kim* had happened before. It was as though the new reign had inspired a new spirit in writers and composers as well as in the British people. Edward Elgar's overture *Cockaigne* embodied the joyous bustle of London traffic, London people, and he was writing his *Coronation Ode* to be performed in honour of the first British coronation in sixty-five years. But the coronation, planned on a magnificent scale, failed to take place as planned on June 26, 1902, for the King had fallen victim to an alarming and painful complaint, diagnosed by his doctors as appendicitis, inflammation of the vermiform appendix, a small, apparently useless, and hitherto unpublicized organ attached to the intestine. An operation to remove it was performed, while the country waited with bated breath. It was successful, the King made a recovery remarkable in view of his age and weight, and the postponed coronation took place on August 9 amid splendid scenes, while crowds dancing and rejoicing in the street sang:

We'll all be merry,
Drinking whisky, wine and sherry.
Let's all be merry
On Coronation Day.

James Bellamy, who had achieved his ambition to become a member of the Household Cavalry, rode proudly in the procession.

Lady Marjorie and Richard were fortunate enough to be invited to a weekend house party at Sandringham, where for many years the King had trained his racehorses and reared the game birds whose mass slaughter provided such sport

KING EDWARD HEARTILY BIDS YOU WELCOME TO HIS CORONATION DINNER, ON JULY 5TH. 1902.

An invitation to a coronation dinner that was postponed because of the King's illness

Long live the King! The coronation procession at Westminster

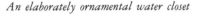
An elaborately ornamental water closet

Shanks's superior bath cabinet

for the nobility and gentry from August 12 onwards every year. It was a huge, rambling, mid-Victorian place, not quite so chilling to the blood as Queen Victoria's residences had been (she disliked any form of heating and would order bedroom fires to be extinguished if she happened to find them burning) but without central heating, a luxury indeed in those days. Bathrooms *en suite* were unthought of, as were hot and cold running water in bedrooms. Ladies' maids and valets might look after all the tedious details of dressing, cleaning, and mending, but a wash was still a matter of a basin and ewer on a washstand and a copper can of hot water with a towel over it. Baths were monumental affairs resembling four-poster beds, like the Shanks's Independent Plunge, Spray and Shower Bath, metallic enamelled inside and japanned outside with a graceful pattern. Four brass taps, one above the other, supplied the various requirements of the bather. America was to give the lead in bathroom improvements, when in 1908 the Statler Hotel in Buffalo startled potential guests with the offer of "A Room with a Bath for a Dollar and a Half."

Sanitary arrangements at Sandringham were as good as could be expected at that date: elaborately ornamented water closets whose plumbing could be guaranteed not to spread disease. King Edward was most careful about such matters. His father, the Prince Consort, had died not of overwork or of worry about his son's behaviour with an Irish actress, as the Queen had declared, but of typhoid fever born of the primitive drainage system at Windsor. In 1871 Edward, then Prince of Wales, was stricken with the same illness while staying at Londesborough Lodge, near Scarborough. He recovered, but his groom and another guest died. Thereafter Edward took a lively interest in drainage, even declaring that if he were not a prince his next preference would be to be a plumber.

Sandringham weekends were not as restful as might be imagined. They involved, for the ladies especially, an exhausting routine of changing their clothes. In the morning a lady might require a riding habit for following the hounds or sporting clothes and sturdy boots in which to go out with the guns, then back to change for lunch. Teatime demanded a different toilette. Then, after a much-needed rest in a loose tea gown, temporarily free from the painful imprisonment of corsets, came the change to full evening dress for dinner— floating tulles, sleek silks and satins, high-piled, elaborately dressed hair, jewellery of an appropriate kind ("no diamonds in the country" was one of Lady Marjorie's dicta), and a serene indifference to the draughts that might assail bare shoulders or arms in transparent sleeves. Should a lady find herself honoured by being seated opposite the King she would need to be perpetually on the alert to maintain a flow of lively conversation. One lapse and the heavy royal eyelids would droop, the plump royal fingers begin to drum on the table. A different wine with each course was the custom, but ladies were not supposed to show any undue interest. Certainly it was not done for a lady to take a second glass of wine at dessert, or, if she were so bold as to want one, the gentleman next to her would fill her glass; on no account should she help herself. "Passing the decanters is principally for the gentlemen," said the books of etiquette. An unwise joke directed at or overheard by the King might have serious consequences; one would never be asked to Sandringham again.

Social stresses made these house-party weekends anything but holidays, which were taken when the London Season was over, Parliament in recess. If the season had been a particularly fatiguing one, the Bellamys might go to South-wold, Lady Marjorie's home in Wiltshire, to get away from the dust and smoke of London. Otherwise, they might spend August in Scotland, shooting with friends, and return with welcome supplies of game for Mrs. Bridges's larder; or cross the Channel to Deauville or Le Touquet. Wherever they went, they would be accompanied by Miss Roberts and Alfred or Mr. Hudson.

(OVERLEAF) *A royal house party at Sandringham, photographed in Commodore Wood on a November afternoon in 1909*

64

Only the rich could take such holidays. The better-off middle class might, if they had the chance, rent a house in the country or by the seaside to which Mama could take the family, while Papa went on working in the City and visited them at weekends. It was considerably cheaper than paying for a large family of children at a boardinghouse. The parents of E. Nesbit's *Four Children* did this and delighted the children of England with their discoveries of the remarkable Psammead, a wonder-working sand fairy whose magic always went wrong. Those who did patronize the establishments of seaside landladies would probably do so only for a week, all the time the wage earner could spare from his work. Seaside bathing was on a very smaller scale and was mainly conducted from bathing huts drawn by horses to the edge of the water. Male bathers wore long-legged one-piece costumes, usually striped, and females were clad from neck to calf in all-enveloping costumes. Modesty, not comfort or beauty, was their first consideration, and those holiday-makers who preferred to recline on

Edward in his element, shooting at Sandringham

The staff enjoys a picnic by the sea.

the crowded beaches would not have dreamed of going hatless or wearing specially light summer clothes. They wore what they wore at other times: high stiff collars, thick materials that soaked up perspiration and made railway carriages unsavoury, dark suits and bowler hats for the men, long-sleeved blouses and trailing skirts for the women. Even the children suffered uncomplainingly in their hot thick clothes. It was an enormous treat to be allowed to peel off one's shoes and stockings and paddle in the sea. The benefits of sunshine were as unknown to these early Edwardians as the existence of vitamins.

A great many of the workers were too poor to be able to afford a holiday at all. These would go for the day to Margate or Ramsgate, Brighton or Blackpool or Southend, in excursion trains at special cheap fares, crowded coachfuls of people

Dressed for a summer's day on the beach at Southsea

determined to eat, drink, and be merry for what might be their one day's outing in the year. The Bellamy servants had at least two such days, the annual spring trip to Kew Gardens and the August Bank Holiday excursion to Clacton, Herne Bay, or one of the other Kentish resorts not too far from London. Because they had generous and considerate employers, they had a fair number of individual days and half-days off and even the occasional week if one of them had been in poor health. Mr. Hudson would go to stay with his sister Fiona, who with her husband Robert Wilson kept a boardinghouse at Eastbourne. Mrs. Bridges very occasionally spent a few days with her sister, married to a prosperous draper and living at Great Yarmouth in Norfolk. "Just for the change," she would make it clear to everybody, for a certain strain had been noticeable in her relationships with her sister and brother-in-law since Gilbert had jilted her to marry the younger and prettier girl. Rose enjoyed going home to Southwold and envied Miss Roberts her privilege of travelling with Lady Marjorie. Poor little Irish Emily never went anywhere; the fare to Ireland was quite beyond her means, and she was not of sufficient importance in the Bellamy household to warrant the family paying for her.

The King himself had gone abroad in August 1901. It was not a holiday, for he was bound to the deathbed of his sister "Vicky," Empress Dowager of Prussia, who of all his brothers and sisters had been closest to him. But Mr. Hudson read something sinister into it, remembering the Kaiser at the Queen's funeral and being alarmed by newspaper reports of the armaments firm of Krupp taking over the Germania shipbuilding yards at Kiel. What could it bode? he wondered. In 1902 he had further cause for disquiet with the laying of the Trans-Pacific cable; all this bringing together of nations could end in nothing but trouble. It was a slight consolation to him that in 1902 the first celebration of Empire Day took place. The Duke and Duchess of York had visited Australia, and King Edward was now ruler of "all the British Dominions beyond the Seas." It was a proud addition to his titles.

Lady Marjorie's dressmaker, who ran a very expensive establishment in Jermyn Street, showed her fashion plates from Paris depicting a refreshingly new look in ladies' clothes. "This is the Russian Tunic, my lady, most flattering—straight to the knees, with a broad belt to emphasise the waist—inspired by the skating costume, of course. For winter it could be charmingly trimmed with fur, but at this time of year—well, a rich beading would look quite delightful."

On the right, the new Russian coat costume

Lady Marjorie succumbed to the tunic's lure and to the pouter-pigeon bosom that was *de règle* both for daytime and evening. And in her attic bedroom Rose, who was handy with a needle, made herself a Russian tunic of cheap but serviceable material, to wear on her days off and when she eventually found herself a Young Man. So far he had not appeared, but she was always hopeful. Marriage to, say, a respectable tradesman or clerk was the only means of escape from a life of domestic service.

Changes were in store for Richard Bellamy, not sartorial but political. In July 1902 the great Lord Salisbury resigned as Prime Minister, to be succeeded by his nephew, Arthur Balfour. Early in 1903 Richard, a personal friend of Balfour's and a warm admirer of his, was given a position in the new Conservative

Growing up in the London slums

Administration. The post afforded him a quiet satisfaction and delighted his wife, who had always considered him insufficiently ambitious for the son-in-law of such a distinguished High Tory as her father. With a Social Revolutionary Party already established in Russia and undercurrents of political unrest in Britain, it was important that the men at the top should be of the right political colour. Undeniably, there were a great many poor people in London; one could not help seeing them as one drove along the Embankment at night, every bench along the route filled with shivering, huddled forms. In the Kennington Road, south of the river, a district Lady Marjorie never visited, the young Charles Chaplin was living with his mother in the garret of a derelict old house. The atmosphere of the room was stifling; smells of cabbage and cats drifted up to it. Charles looked out of the dirty window at the crowded London roofs and dreamed dreams of the jolly life his father had led as a music-hall artist, a "vaudevillian." The boy was only one of a multitude living in utter squalor— and utter boredom for less lively minds than his, for many of the poor could not even read, and wireless and television were undreamed of. There was so little to do except drink.

However, there were other things to occupy the minds of politicians besides the plight of the poor, who, as they reminded themselves from the Scriptures, we have always with us. The South African war was at last over, and the mess remained to clear up. Richard, and the government in which he served, set out to tackle the job, and King Edward prepared for extensive travels in 1903 that would earn him the affectionate title of Peacemaker.

At the Savoy Theatre, home of the Gilbert and Sullivan operas, a new work called *Merrie England* was produced, a tuneful tale of love and intrigue in the reign of Queen Elizabeth. There was the Virgin Queen herself, awesome in a shimmer of jewels and a towering, pearl-encrusted red wig, her courtier Walter Raleigh out of favour with her for falling in love with her lady-in-waiting, a wealth of charming songs—and the Yeomen of England.

> *For nations to eastward and nations to westward*
> *As foemen might curse them, the Yeomen of England,*
> *No other land can nurse them*
> *But their mother-land, old England;*
> *And on her broad bosom shall they ever thrive.*

It was just the entertainment for the times, people agreed.

A working-class home in London in the early 1900s

72

A guide for the house parlourmaid

CHAPTER FOUR

The New Woman

Early in 1903 Kate, the under-house parlourmaid at No. 165, disgraced herself. Overfamiliarity with a soldier home from South Africa who was full of romantic stories about his exploits in that far land led to what was sometimes known as a Little Consequence or a Little Mistake.

All her life Lady Marjorie had been familiar with servant girls' Little Mistakes. Annie Besant's campaigns in the last decades of the century had made a little—just a little—difference to the population rate in Britain and even America, where Anthony Comstock's Society for the Suppression of Vice withheld knowledge of birth-control methods from American women for forty-two years, undoing much of Annie Besant's good work. But the primitive hush-hush contraception practised in the early 1900s was not available to unmarried women, especially of the lower orders.

Queen Victoria had been notably, and surprisingly, generous in her judgement of unfortunate girls. But Lady Marjorie had no intention of emulating the late Queen on this occasion. Kate was called before her, quietly reprimanded for her foolishness, and sent home to her mother in Lambeth with five pounds—a small fortune to such a girl, the staff agreed.

Kate's replacement, the girl who called herself Clemence Dumas, though her real surname was Moffat, came to them with false references, forged by the manageress of the registry office to which she had applied for employment.

Leisure time in the servants' quarters

Employers were clearly warned against such agencies in the household manuals of the day:

> *While there are offices of high standing, where business is done in an honest and upright manner, there are many others whose dealings can by no means be relied upon.*

Very fortunately for Clemence, renamed Sarah as being more suitable for a servant, Lady Marjorie did not investigate the references or the girl's background. Had she done so, the awful truth would have come out: Sarah had been in prison for the "crime" of being caught assisting a fraudulent spiritualist medium. Under the Vagrancy Act, Sarah was sentenced to a month in Holloway Prison.

It was a bitter humiliation to a lively, ambitious girl. There had been the compulsory bath, the medical examination, the confiscation of personal possessions. The prison uniform was a drab dress of coarse serge; the cell was twelve feet long by seven feet wide, the bed was a plank with a mattress and two blankets, the prisoners' only reading a Bible, prayerbook, and hymnbook. Their diet consisted of solid starch: for breakfast, bread; for midday dinner, an oatmeal gruel known as stirabout; for supper, bread again. Later in the sentence they were allowed suet pudding or potatoes for dinner and extra gruel for breakfast. This diet the prison officers considered "sufficient and nourishing . . . thoroughly wholesome . . . the very great latitude in the substitutes provides that variety of feeding so necessary to health." In fact, one women's magazine claimed "a course of prison treatment . . . may be recommended as superior to a visit to any health resort on the Continent for building up one's constitution and generally restoring health." It is to be doubted whether the King's lady friends, taking the cure at Baden, would have agreed.

There was a shadow over this early Edwardian England, the growing, threatening shadow of Germany, ruled by the King's power-hungry nephew. Thus the young Baron Klaus von Rimmer brought disruption into the Bellamy household when Elizabeth, back from Dresden, introduced him into the family as a house guest. Was he, in fact, a member of a banking family, studying business in the City? Or, as seemed more likely, an agent or spy for one of the great international arms firms? Firms like Krupp, Vickers, and Skoda, who were amassing fortunes as they outdid each other in the manufacture of weapons

Women working in the kitchen of Holloway Prison

for the next war, a war many people could scent in the still peaceful air of Edwardian England. There were strange rumours of Germans working in England in perfectly ordinary jobs—barbers, waiters, shop assistants—who were really spies for Germany.

Richard Bellamy, in his reports to the Committee of Imperial Defence, expressed his unease about the outbreak of the Russo-Japanese War and even more so about tidings that Kaiser Wilhelm was pressing the Tsar of Russia, cousin to the Duke of York, and sufficiently like him to be taken for his twin brother, to form a league with France and Germany against Britain.

Admiral von Tirpitz was rumoured, correctly, to be building a mighty fleet with which the Kaiser intended to rival Britain's naval power, so long supreme. Most Englishmen felt the steady growth of the German fleet had only one

Japanese infantry

An American view of the Russo-Japanese War

object, not the security of Germany but a contest for command of the seas. But, as statesmen were beginning to agree, Britain had the strongest of diplomatic weapons in her own King. In his long years as Prince of Wales, kicking his heels in idleness, Edward had become a familiar figure in France but in a strictly private capacity. He loved France and Paris in particular; had visited it many times, more or less incognito, a sophisticated boulevardier completely at home in that most sophisticated of cities. He had had mistresses among its women, the black-gloved, black-stockinged actresses, dancers, and *cocottes*: Jane Avril, the ugly-beautiful creature who appeared in so many of Toulouse-Lautrec's drawings, Liane de Pougy from Provence, Sarah Bernhardt of the cloudy hair and smouldering eyes, a bevy of enchantresses foreshadowing those girls of Maxim's celebrated by *The Merry Widow*'s Prince Danilo who sings of "Lolo, Dodo, Jou-Jou, Clo-Clo, Margot, Frou-Frou." Frivolous Paris of the can-can and the champagne drunk from tiny slippers had welcomed Edward as Prince of Wales.

Then the Boer War had come, and French newspapers had attacked Queen Victoria and Britain in general. French imperial ambitions clashed with those of Britain; there were envy and malice and fear in the air. It was time someone with sufficient diplomacy stepped in, and Edward was the man for the hour. Wily as any Renaissance monarch, he delicately ascertained that at least two French political leaders, President Loubet and Théophile Delcassé, would like to see France and Britain better friends. So Edward, after highly successful meetings with the kings of Portugal and Italy, decided to arrange a state visit to Paris, against the advice of his ministers, who in any case were not consulted until it was too late for them to take any action.

His reception by the French Head of State was warm. The crowds were less enthusiastic. With supreme aplomb, Edward appeared to mistake the jeers and boos for shouts of welcome. The more they booed, the more graciously he smiled and bowed. It was a policy that could not fail to succeed, and in a matter of days he had won over the heart of Paris. The Entente Cordiale had begun, proving the worth of Edward's highly personal policy of combining business with pleasure, which was to earn him the titles of "the Uncle of Europe" and "the Peacemaker."

In 1905 Arthur Balfour resigned as Prime Minister. For months he had been fighting disunity in the Conservative Party, largely over the question of tariff reform. It seemed a change for the worse. Balfour had dealt brilliantly with the tangled skeins of foreign affairs; under him Britain held a position of strength abroad such as it had not held for half a century. But there was too much opposition to him on home matters for him to remain. The new Liberal Prime Minister, Sir Henry Campbell-Bannerman, was a sincere, clear-sighted man not afraid to speak his mind and devoted to his party.

James Bellamy was enjoying himself in the Life Guards, that hand-picked

"The Divine Sarah"

squadron reserved for ceremonial duties. There was always "something doing," some royal occasion to attend. The Guards received admiring stares when riding beside the King's carriage in scarlet uniforms glittering with gold thread, the sun glinting back from shining breastplates, white plumes nodding on their helmets, white gauntlets on their hands, the helmet strap in regulation position beneath the lower lip.

Then there were the King's Evening Courts, in which a bevy of beautiful girls (some of them American "Dollar Princesses") were presented to royalty in the traditional costume, with its train of standard length, long white gloves, and cluster of white feather plumes worn on a headband, as if to echo the Life Guards' uniform. There were dancing and flirtation and laughter and champagne and, after the presentation ceremony, a formal procession of the royal party through a lane of debutantes and their mothers or chaperones, each bending her knee in a sweeping curtsey. Amidst so much beauty Queen Alexandra shone out superbly. No longer young (she was a grandmother several times over), she had retained her perfect figure and proud carriage and her porcelain complexion. She could wear anything without looking overdressed: jewels and spangles by day if she felt so inclined; jackets scintillating with sequins of the colours she loved, Imperial purple and violet; more violets, made of velvet and wire, clustering on her charming little head. Her daughter-in-law the Princess of Wales, who had been Princess May of Teck, was a very different figure. She was upright as a soldier, rigidly corseted, severe of expression; her watchword was dignity. To save the Princess the trouble of fittings, her clothes were always tried on a

Presentation at Court

The Princess of Wales

Queen Alexandra

dressmaker's dummy made to her measurements, and she appeared to ignore fashion, wearing garments as far removed as possible from the frivolity and glitter of those of her charming mother-in-law. Later in life she would become almost a figure of caricature in her squarish, tailored coats and skirts, flat shoes, pouter-pigeon bosom, and the invariable toque on her rigidly waved hair.

In fact, the dress of both ladies was dictated by their husbands. King Edward liked his women as feminine as possible; the Prince of Wales' taste was conservative and dull. The Princess did not venture to wear a colour or a style

Lady Marjorie and Captain Hammond of the Khyber Rifles

disapproved of by her husband. Even when skirts became shorter and she, who had beautiful legs, hoped to be able to reveal a little more of them than had previously been seen, a lady-in-waiting had to test George's reaction first by shortening her own skirts. The royal seal of approval was not forthcoming. The lady's dress was "too short." Next day its hem had been let down again, and the Princess Mary's remained at floor-length.

Except for his ceremonial duties, James hardly ever moved in such high circles, but it was he who introduced his mother to Captain Hammond of the Khyber Rifles. The brief, ecstatic affair that blazed up between them was the only excursion into infidelity of Lady Marjorie's life. Captain Hammond was an utterly exotic element in the well-oiled, predictable cycle of life in Eaton Place, coming as he did from a world of torrid heat, strange sights and smells, gorgeous temples, and a squalid poverty outdoing the worst of London's slums.

His life was that of the imperial Raj, of complacent, omnipotent Sahibs, and of their ladies, languidly gossiping in claustrophobic hill stations, their children in faraway England at boarding school, or, as Kipling had been, unhappily fostered. It was the India whose Imperial crown Disraeli had won for Queen Victoria; the India of Kipling's wonderful stories, seething with a discontent

Kipling's India

nobody quite perceived as yet, the struggle of Eastern culture against that of the West. Lord Curzon, Viceroy since 1898, had created the North-West Frontier province to bring something like peace to that unruly border, had reformed drainage, had cut some of the red tape that choked the Civil Service, had tried to level out the differences between white man and brown; and, after a dispute with Lord Kitchener, one of the heroes of South Africa, he had resigned office in 1905. Nobody in that year could have predicted what would happen in the lifetime of some of them: the end of the British Raj and the self-government of India. To the Edwardians, India was "the brightest jewel in the Empire's crown."

Elizabeth Bellamy, nineteen and a rebel, reacted against the correct behaviour instilled into a young lady at a finishing school and allowed herself to be influenced into sympathy with Suffragism. The New Woman affected a characteristic style of dress, a severe coat and skirt costume with a high collar. Quite often these ladies also donned a mannish, Homburg-type hat and spectacles. The cartoonists revelled in this unalluring image. Conventional ladies were shocked and repelled at the interest shown by these New Women in such unfeminine, dangerous persons as the Russian-American Emma Goldman, the self-confessed anarchist against whose like President Roosevelt was waging war. All England had been shocked by news of the Russian revolution following "Bloody Sunday" and the rise of Trotsky. Could the New Woman not realise where violent social changes were leading? Queen Victoria had exerted herself to keep women out of the professions, and Queen Alexandra was surely an example of the Womanly Woman to be copied by all her subjects.

In fact, only a small proportion of women really supported Emmeline Pankhurst and her Women's Social and Political Union. Literature directed at women was full of fictional examples of young girls traduced by other women (mostly older and plainer, for a large number of suffragettes were spinsters or widows) into working for a Cause with which they felt no real identification. Only a few years earlier there had been a rather colourful short story in that respectable magazine *The Housewife* about a sweet young girl, Cassandra Tripp, whose widowed mother had been a fanatic supporter of women's rights, adamant that her daughter should not marry the handsome editor of the *Weekly Satirist*, in which anti-feminist views were regularly aired. Cassandra herself thought that "there are lots of women who would not know what to do with the vote if they had it. I should not, for one." And, very wisely acting on her

"Elizabeth Bellamy, nineteen and a rebel"

mother's statement at a public meeting that "every woman has a right to decide as she will," she ran away with her editor and lived happily ever after.

Yet many women, without being militant extremists, were working for a bigger place in the social system, and some were getting it. One of the only subjects on which Queen Victoria had agreed with Mr. Gladstone was that women ought to be kept out of the professions, particularly the "Medical Line." According to Longford's biography of the Queen, she regarded it as an *"awful idea . . .* allowing *young girls* and young men to enter the dissecting room together." But in 1883 Elizabeth Garrett Anderson, the first woman to qualify in medicine in Britain, became Dean of the London School of Medicine for Women, and by 1901 there were over 200 women doctors in practise and over 100 women dentists. The vote was refused to women partly on the ground that they could express their political views through their husbands. But (quite apart from the fact that husband's and wife's views might be quite different) many

George Bernard Shaw

women had no husband to speak for them. Maiden aunts abounded, left over from those large Victorian families that seemed so often to consist mainly of girls; and today's New Woman was not always anxious to marry.

The very institution of marriage, once regarded as a holy estate, was being questioned. Bernard Shaw frequently reversed or altered the "traditional" order. His Ann Whitefield of *Man and Superman* (1903) is an agent of the Life Force, capturing and marrying her man in spite of himself—a distinct change in the accepted roles. One of the characters in *Getting Married* (1908) wonders "who will begin the stand against marriage? It must come some day." In *Misalliance* (1910) Shaw shocked theatregoers by allowing his Hypatia Tarleton to ask her father to buy the young pilot, Joey Percival, for her—otherwise he will not be able to afford to marry her. H. G. Wells's novel *Ann Veronica* (1909) was banned from some libraries because its independent heroine ran away from her suburban home to elope with a married man. "I want to be a person by myself, and to pull my own strings. . . . "

Edwardian ladies' magazines were ever helpful in suggestions as to "what we should do with our girls." They were not, on the whole, very adventurous, inclining to recommend such money-making crafts as millinery, cookery, and metalwork, but a *Lady's Realm* of the early 1900s went so far as to instruct its readers in the technique and opportunities of Sanitary Inspecting. The article was accompanied by a sketch of an elegant young creature in a kind of shepherdess costume, bouquet in hand, daintily crossing a stream—or possibly a drain.

At the same time that women were turning away from their traditional role, fundamental questions about the nature of sexuality were appearing, as in the works of the Viennese psychoanalyst, Sigmund Freud. In 1900 he had published his *Traumdeutung*, a treatise on the interpretation of dreams. It was very far in content from those Dream Books that Mrs. Bridges and her kind enjoyed ("To dream of a black cat means an enemy will cross your path," "To dream of a wedding portends a funeral"). It delved into that hitherto unknown territory, the subconscious, and produced monsters. In the following year came his *Psychopathology of Everyday Life*, another work that Edwardian mothers would have considered very shocking. But only the erudite or the medically trained read it at this time. It would be years before people talked freely (and usually inaccurately) about the ego, the id, the libido, repression, and the Oedipus Complex.

Miss Camille Clifford

CHAPTER FIVE

The Wheels of Change

Political and international troubles rumbled in the background, but Edwardian life went its own cheerful way. The old Gaiety Theatre, where Victorian burlesque had flourished, had been demolished to make way for a new thoroughfare, Aldwych, sweeping in a semicircle from the Strand, where a wilderness of slums had been. In its place a new Gaiety had risen, built by the great impresario George Edwardes, known in the profession as "the Guv'nor." When the new theatre opened in 1903 the occasion was a splendid one. King Edward and Queen Alexandra occupied the Royal Box; the cream of fashionable and frivolous London filled the stalls and circle. James Bellamy was there with his friend "Bunny" Newbury, picking out the prettiest girls in the chorus as likely partners for supper afterwards.

The musical comedy was *The Orchid*, starring George Grossmith Junior and the lovely Gertie Millar, one of the most popular of the "Gaiety Girls," whose pretty faces, luxuriant hair, and incredibly small waists adorned so many postcards; others were Gabrielle Ray, Lily Elsie (the first "Merry Widow" to charm London in 1907), Marie Studholme, and the beautiful sisters Phyllis and Zena Dare. A musical comedy also performed in 1903 was Ivan Caryll's *The Earl and the Girl*, a title highly applicable to many of these beauties of the theatre, not a few of whom married into the aristocracy.

An American, Miss Camille Clifford, was the original "Gibson Girl," popularizing a remarkable feminine figure—the waist tight-laced to an incredible smallness, eighteen inches or so, the bosom pushed out and the rear jutting backwards, giving an effect of an hourglass bending in the middle. Somehow, the much-entertained ladies of the stage managed to retain their elegant, unnatural outlines, in spite of the amount of food Edwardians were expected to consume. The American cartoonist Charles Dana Gibson made many drawings of the early "pin-ups" (the "Gibson Girls"), immortalizing their extraordinary silhouettes. Miss Clifford herself was daringly photographed in negligee, coyly displaying the immense length of her stay laces. Rich young men collected such

Edwardian Ascot

pictures avidly and quite frequently collected the ladies as well, escorting them to such fashionable restaurants as Rule's, the Savoy, and the Café Royal, sweeping them off to the July regatta at Henley-on-Thames for the great boating event of the Season and treating them to deliciously naughty little dinners at the famous riverside hotel Skindles' at nearby Maidenhead, sometimes even to the occasional naughty night there. The author Jerome K. Jerome, whose book *Three Men in a Boat* humourously described a journey up the Thames, looked down on Maidenhead as "the town of shabby hotels, patronised chiefly by dudes and ballet girls . . . the *London Journal* duke always had his 'little place' at Maidenhead; and the heroine of the three-volume novel always dines there when she goes out on the spree with somebody else's husband." But at this distance in time from the days of the Edwardian Henley Regatta, it seems an alluring pageant of bright colours, women in gorgeous clothes, men for once abandoning their dark suits for white flannels, brilliantly striped blazers, and straw hats. The same cheerful scenes took place at Ascot, at the Eton and Harrow cricket match at Lord's, and in Cowes Week, the annual regatta held at the end of the Season under the auspices of the Royal Yacht Squadron. Once the Edwardian era had passed, these events would never be quite the same again.

In 1906 the Bellamys at last decided to take the plunge and buy a motorcar. Arthur Balfour had owned one as early as 1902, and Richard had contemplated with some interest his arrival in it at the House of Commons. What should they buy? Herbert Austin was already manufacturing cars, and two years earlier C. S. Rolls had first become interested in the fine cars being built by H. Royce. In 1906 the firm of Rolls-Royce was founded, and in due course one of their cars would seem the obvious choice for a family like the Bellamys. But the car they chose at the Motor Show at Olympia was a Renault, the model His Majesty had also bought that year. It was beautifully built and could actually travel at forty-five miles an hour; its colour was a dignified royal blue.

They made another concession to modernity in having their house wired for electric light. This had taken place during August and September, when they themselves would be out of town, for the noise and mess involved were fearful. Mr. Hudson and the other servants left behind had to put up with it, alarming though the whole thing seemed to them. Mrs. Bridges and Rose approached the light switches with the utmost caution and, like many other Edwardians, continued to light their way to bed with a candle.

It was a year of progress, this 1906. Amundsen, the Norwegian explorer,

King Edward VII in his first motorcar

Dreadnought

completed his voyage through the Northwest Passage, fixing the position of the North Magnetic Pole. H. M. S. *Dreadnought* was launched—the first modern battleship, with a speed of 21 knots; and the Cunard liner *Lusitania* made her first voyage, none aboard dreaming how tragic would be her last one in 1915. The Simplon Tunnel was opened, linking Switzerland and Italy for the convenience of travellers. Perhaps they would visit Florence next year, said Lady Marjorie, and enjoy this new wonder of science. Nearer home, two more London Underground lines were opened, Bakerloo and Piccadilly.

"The world is growing smaller every minute, Mrs. Bridges," observed Mr. Hudson, laying down his paper with an air of gloom. "I don't like it at all. If the Almighty had meant us to fly He would have given us wings, and if He had meant us to travel under the earth we should have come into the world as giant moles."

Mrs. Bridges tried to envisage this phenomenon, but her mind, as she put it, boggled. She reached for her recipe book and began to carry out Lady Marjorie's instructions for the menus of the day.

Lady Marjorie and Lady Prue dutifully attended a performance of the opera *The Wreckers* by the woman composer Ethel Smyth but found the music discordant and unpleasing—unwomanly, in a word. They were not surprised to hear that Miss Smyth was an ardent suffragette. "The old Queen was perfectly right in wishing to keep women out of the professions," said Lady Prue, "if that's the sort of thing they produce."

They, and the many others who read it, were better pleased with John Galsworthy's novel *The Man of Property*. Galsworthy, a wealthy man who had shown no great literary promise so far, was newly married to the woman who had been his cousin Arthur's wife. Those who knew them, and basked in the popularity the book won for itself, said that Ada Galsworthy was the inspiration not only for the novel but for the character of Irene, whose unfaithfulness to her husband, Soames Forsyte, produced a reaction the violence of which agreeably

Mrs. Bridges boggled

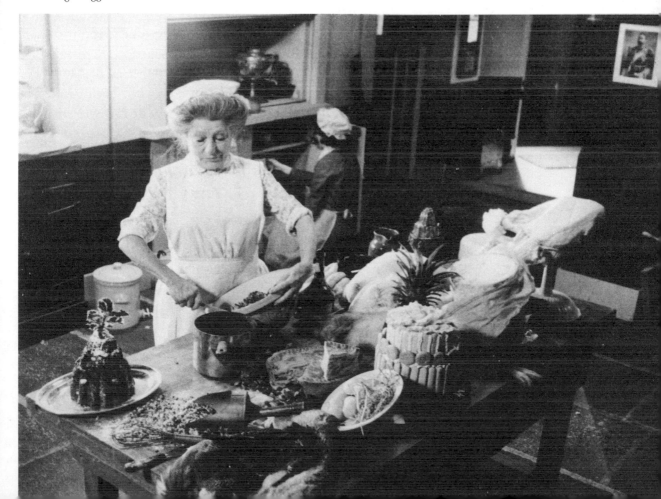

shocked readers. Galsworthy had written about a family, the Forsytes, who were the sort of people he knew from the inside; Old Jolyon was in part a portrait of his own father. The book proved to be the first in the series of novels which became famous as *The Forsyte Saga*.

But Galsworthy did not follow it up with another Forsyte book until 1918, when he produced *The Indian Summer of a Forsyte*. Perhaps, emerging when it did into a world weary of war, it was a kind of "Upstairs, Downstairs" of its day, reflecting an age gone by that seemed leisured and restful in the extreme compared with the stress of modern times. It covered almost the same period as the Bellamy saga, the last part, *On Forsyte Change*, being published in 1930. In the 1960s it was to travel the world through the medium of television.

In an England that was still the England of the Forsytes, an architecture that would be called Edwardian was emerging. Blocks of mansion flats were springing up in London, usually of red brick and vaguely baroque in style; flat-dwelling was becoming more and more the accepted thing. Large buildings in general were even larger, for new structural materials, such as structural steel, just being introduced allowed a freedom of planning previously impossible. Slum clearance, such as had taken place in Aldwych, was replacing ancient crumbling buildings with new, imposing ones. The terrible overcrowding in such areas as Whitechapel was being eased by the erection of flats for the working classes. They were designed and put up at the behest of the London County Council and other local bodies, to whom power had been granted by Acts of Parliament in the 1890s. As the first borough-built flats were rising, a number of enlightened and wealthy employers were laying out housing estates for their workers: rows of small houses or somewhat larger homes, with pleasant gardens, space for vegetable allotments, and paved roads with grass borders. Lord Southwold's tenants in Wiltshire continued to live in their old cottages, very little modernized, in conditions much the same as they had been in the eighteenth century, but other workers, like those at Port Sunlight in Cheshire and Cadbury's Bournville, were more fortunate. These industrial estates were to be followed in 1903 by the first Garden City at Letchworth, Hertfordshire, and a year or two later by Hampstead Garden Suburb. Divided from Hampstead Heath and Village by a road running along the top of the Heath, this was a most pleasant place of neat little houses, each with its own garden, in which working people might live and pay rents they could afford, with all the amenities of the country, yet just a short tube journey away from Charing Cross and the City.

Bank holiday on Hampstead Heath

There was little thought in the minds of those who planned and built these idyllic small houses that in half a century all the "working people" would have gone, their dwellings sought after by people from every rank and profession, including the very rich, who built large houses for themselves around the nucleus of the original suburb.

The Bellamys would be unlikely to know anyone in Hampstead Garden Suburb, or in Welwyn Garden City, farther out in Hertfordshire. Their servants might spend a Sunday afternoon or a Bank Holiday on Hampstead Heath, with drinks at those famous inns, the Spaniards or the Bull and Bush of popular song, but they would get no nearer the suburb, whose dwellers were free, not tied, like themselves, to a house and in particular a basement. They were not in touch on any level with that layer of society that was neither Upstairs nor Downstairs: the middle classes.

There had been a middle class of a sort for centuries, of course, though unacknowledged as such. At one time doctors and the humbler clergymen were reckoned among them. They could rise in the world by marrying above their station, but to the Upstairs man of the eighteenth and early nineteenth centuries, the Lord Southwold of his time, there was little to choose in social status between the country physician who would come bowling up to the hall in his gig or pony cart, the lawyer who would be sent for when His Lordship furiously decided to disinherit his eldest son, and the domestic staff at the hall. There was a legend about an eighteenth-century countess to the effect that she would never stoop to address her doctor directly but would give her instructions through a servant. "Tell the surgeon that he may now bleed the Countess of Carlisle."

The Industrial Revolution had changed all that, making small men—civil engineers, architects, brewers—rich through their contribution to technical

Edwardian middle-class family life

progress. The Prince Consort, with his passion for technology and reform in living conditions, had given them further scope. Cotton mills, railways, blast furnaces, factories, new industrial towns made ordinary men richer even than the upper classes, who would still not have dreamed of inviting a grocer or a draper to dinner, however wealthy such men might be. Mrs. Bridges's brother-in-law was one of these, having built a chain of drapers' shops in the Midlands from small beginnings, but when he and his family rose in the world, and his daughter married a merchant whose name was to become as famous as that of Liberty, Whiteley, or Tiffany in America, Mrs. Bridges would use the servants' entrance when visiting them, if, indeed, she visited them at all.

By the early 1900s the small man employed by the greater might enjoy a reasonable prosperity, provided he worked hard and maintained his respectability. He would live outside central London, in Putney, Ealing, or Wimbledon, where Hazel Bellamy's parents lived—districts looked down on by the hereditary upper classes as "suburban." The respectable middle class was exemplified by Hazel's mother, Mrs. Forrest, a churchgoing, whist-playing Conservative. Left-wing intellectuals of the middle classes existed in large numbers, but a modest civil servant like Mr. Forrest would have nothing to do with them. He would mow his small lawn on a Saturday afternoon, take a walk in the nearby open country—Wimbledon Common, perhaps, or along Thames-side. His wife would not employ a living-in servant, for the days were gone when every middle-class family, however poor themselves, would keep a young servant to do the rough work. Dickens' Mrs. Micawber had her servant-maid, the young Copperfields their series of disaster-prone domestics. Now these were gone. Only the "upper" middle classes would keep servants in the spacious houses they were building farther out in the country and in the new suburbs, and such servants would have a degree of freedom not enjoyed by those of Belgravia, whose life-styles were indeed limited.

When little Irish Emily fell in love with a wealthy woman's footman, his employer threatened to sack the young man without references, and Emily was accordingly informed that a marriage between them was impossible and that she must put William out of her mind. Driven to desperation, the poor girl committed suicide by hanging. She was only one of many who had done so. Friendless, living on a pittance, with no prospect but a life of slavery, a servant such as Emily would never obtain promotion. When she grew too old to work,

David Lloyd George
in 1908

she would be turned away to fend for herself, unless her employers were more than usually kindhearted. It was the Liberal government, returned in the landslide election of 1906, that set about reforming the conditions of such people. The fiery Welshman David Lloyd George, who would soon be Chancellor of the Exchequer, was the spearhead of reform, seeing himself as a kind of Red Cross station for the underprivileged. "I am in a hurry," he declaimed, "for I can hear the moaning of the wounded, and I want to carry relief to them in the alleys, the homes where they lie desolate."

Under this government schoolchildren profited by school meals; for the first time in history they could be sure of at least one square meal a day, barefoot and ragged though many of them might be. Medical inspections were introduced, to nip ailments and diseases in the bud. England would soon be a healthier country. And for the old people, Lloyd George introduced state pensions. They came like a miracle to ageing folk whose only refuge would at one time have been the dreaded workhouse, where husbands and wives were separated and one's declining years were lived out in gruelling hard work and humiliation. No wonder the old people said of the Chancellor, "God bless Lord George!" They felt that such a munificent politician must be a lord at the very least.

Nature-study class in an elementary school in the early 1900s

"The London policeman's day was a long one. . . ."

CHAPTER SIX

To Set
Before
a King

Emily's suicide was one of the causes of the extraordinary aberration that impelled Mrs. Bridges to snatch a baby from its pram and take it back to 165 Eaton Place. The police were called, and things did not look good for Mrs. Bridges. But Mr. Hudson saved the day. Going before the magistrate with her, he explained that since she was "a very lonely person with no relatives or dependents, she had come to regard the dead girl as her own daughter. They were very close." This statement served to put the court in sympathy with Mrs. Bridges' plight, but his next caused Mrs. Bridges to flush red and created such a stir with the denizens of Downstairs that it was the topic of conversation for weeks to come. "She has no one to care for and nobody to care for her. . . . We are both single persons, Your Worship, and it occurred to me that, if I could undertake to keep the accused lady happy and cared for in the future, Your Worship might see his way to overlooking this unfortunate lapse and be assured that . . . such a thing would not occur again." Downstairs was surprised when Mr. Hudson proposed to Mrs. Bridges, but all knew that their marriage would have to be postponed until they both retired from service. For some obscure reason a married pair of servants was not acceptable in London, though in the country it might have been. Such conventions stretched back so far in time that it would have been hard for Lady Marjorie to explain how they originated. She could only have said that the presence of a married couple on the staff might have "caused trouble."

Mrs. Bridges had once been "walking out" with a young policeman. Had she married him she would have led a lonely life, for the London policeman's day was a long one and he was allowed only one day off in fourteen. But she and her family might have been accommodated not in a "section house" belonging to the police station (these were only for single policemen) but in one of the better types of working-class apartment blocks. Her husband would have had to be prepared for any duty from the taking up of stray dogs to answering the bewildered questions of visitors to London, including those hordes in grey cloth caps and mufflers who descended on London for the Soccer Cups Finals. Football mania had already invaded England.

The policeman had a pleasanter time at Lord's and the Oval cricket ground, where, officially on duty, he might watch the brilliant, modest batsman Jack Hobbs, the captainship of C. B. Fry, the amazing versatility of Wilfred Rhodes. Such days in the sun helped to make up for tedious nights of prowling the streets in search of marauders, keeping an eye open for disorderly public houses and for unlit bicycles on the public highway. Until the suffragette movement became strongly militant there would be little real violence for him to quell. He would be most at risk in the dark, fetid streets of Whitechapel, Hoxton, Stepney, and those dockland districts where fights broke out continually between drunken sailors and other inhabitants of such perilous roads as the Ratcliff Highway. Here it would be no unusual thing for a policeman, alone on his beat, to attempt to stop a fight and to be stabbed or kicked unconscious. Drink was the greatest problem in the poor districts. Those who lived a whole family to a room in the filthy tenements of the yet undemolished slums had no other comfort or pleasure. For a few pence they could buy forgetfulness, a feeling of well-being, something to blot out the realities of their drab lives. There were those who condemned the tenement dwellers for spending what little money they had on drink instead of on food and clothing for themselves and their wives and children. "Is it the style that makes the pig, or the pig that makes the style?" asked the cynical. The policeman, who had to deal with the results of violent drunkenness, must sometimes have asked himself the same question as he surveyed the lines of ragged, blank-faced people shuffling into soup kitchens such as the one in which James Bellamy rediscovered Sarah, a disgraced servant who had been reduced to poverty since she left the house in Eaton Place.

Sarah's return to the Bellamy family coincided with a time when housework was rapidly becoming easier. In 1908 the first *Daily Mail* Ideal Home Exhibi-

Royal Ediswan Gasfilled Lamps
" . . . make a welcome lightness
both in the home and in the electric
light bill."

tion was held, displaying to astonished and delighted housewives such work-savers as gas ovens (in their early form), electric fires and kettles, and a vacuum cleaner small enough to be manipulated by one person. This and the carpet sweeper (a rotating brush encased in a flat wooden box on wheels) were to replace the tedious kneeling and hand-sweeping of carpets that had been the house-maid's dreary task before their invention. But for some years the vacuum cleaner would be too costly for use in the houses of people less wealthy than the Bellamys. Rose, like other servants of a conservative nature, dreaded having to handle anything connected with electricity and distrusted the new gadget on sight. But electricity was a minor wonder compared with the news that the first British military airship flight was being made over London. The staff in the basement rushed up the area steps to see it; those upstairs, hearing the news, thrust their heads out of windows. There it went, the fat cigar-shaped thing, gliding majestically through the clouds, above the chimneys and their smoke, a messenger of change and (if they had known it) of doom.

An army balloon at Aldershot

"It's against nature!" cried Mrs. Bridges. The two new young maids clung together in terror, convinced that the monster would fall out of the skies at any moment. Mr. Hudson, frowning, followed its progress. "Count von Zeppelin is said to be building hundreds the like of that," he said. "A whole fleet, to send against us when the time comes."

"Oh, do give over, Mr. Hudson!" said Rose impatiently. "As if it wasn't bad enough, things like that going over London. It ought not to be allowed."

They had read about its coming in the paper that morning. One of the advantages of living in 1908 was that there were so many things to read—if one *could* read. There were over twenty national morning newspapers and nine evening. Alfred Harmsworth, the newspaper magnate who became the first Viscount Northcliffe, had launched the *Daily Mail* and the *Daily Mirror*, aimed at the mass of readers who liked their news delivered in a simple, straightforward manner. Like his *Answers*, they were intended for "the great new generation that is being turned out by the Board Schools, the young men and women who can just read, but are incapable of sustained attention"—in fact, a readership typified by the servant classes. The Northcliffe motto was "explain, simplify, clarify," with plenty of human interest, verbal colour, current talking points, sports news. He bought the more high-minded *Times* and *Observer*, gave

The "Nell Gwynne" hat

them an injection of new life; the literate Mr. Hudson was devoted to *The Times*, always glancing at its headlines before he bore it into the morning room on a silver tray.

Women were catered to in special features; they were shown, by drawings and photographs, how to copy the clothes made fashionable by actresses, such as Julia Neilson's "Nell Gwynne" hat, the Camille Clifford coiffure, the Billie Burke shoe, the Trilby military coat and buttons (the play made from George du Maurier's novel had been revived again and again, fascinating audiences as Trilby herself was fascinated into stardom by the sinister musician Svengali).

Lawrence Kirbridge and Elizabeth Bellamy on their wedding day

The *Sporting Times* or "Pink 'Un" was "written by men for men . . . full of good, clean, wholesome fun," and those who liked their fun more sophisticated might find it in *Punch*.

Through such monthly magazines as the popular *Strand* the writings of authors great and small reached a public that would otherwise not have discovered them. In the *English Review* were to be found the wonderful early poems of John Masefield. Walter de la Mare was writing, as were John Davidson, Thomas Hardy, Alfred Noyes—all visionaries and romantics. The young poet Lawrence Kirbridge, with whom Elizabeth Bellamy fell in love, was far from typical of them. Belonging to a later generation, he seems to have moulded his highly coloured style on the poems of the once-popular Swinburne (who was to die in the next year, 1909) and the young Rupert Brooke. It was a flamboyant, artificial style, with little depth or feeling behind it, and was just the sort of thing to ensnare the rather unsophisticated Elizabeth into a marriage that proved to be disastrous.

But before this romantic mistake, Elizabeth's energies found an outlet in her return to the cause of Women's Suffrage. The suffragettes had had great hopes when the Liberals came into power; the Tories had a reputation for being anti-feminist, whereas Asquith and Lloyd George and the youthful, brilliant Winston Churchill were men of progress.

The women were disappointed. The Liberals proved no more sympathetic to the women's cause than had the previous government. Demonstrations began. Organized by the Pankhursts, mother and daughter, the Northerner Annie Kenney, Lady Constance Lytton, and others, the militant women displayed

The young poet
Rupert Brooke

Suffragette procession, Hyde Park, June 21, 1908

posters in the street, wrote slogans on walls, held public meetings, and when, after defying the police, they were arrested, they often chose to go to prison rather than pay a fine. In the Second Division, where they usually found themselves, they were forced to wear rough prison clothes and submit to the indignities inflicted on ordinary, non-political prisoners. Reports of these humiliations won them much publicity and some sympathy. They won more sympathy when their refusal to accept prison food led to their being forcibly fed liquids through tubes—a painful process formerly carried out only on lunatics.

Then they began to harass government ministers. Churchill and Lloyd George, who might have been their allies, were alienated. A bomb was planted in Lloyd George's home, where it did considerable damage. A girl chained herself to the railings of 10 Downing Street, shouting "Votes for women!" and

Intimations of a lost cause

Emmeline Pankhurst and her daughter in prison,
May 22, 1908

Emmeline Pankhurst attempted an attack on Buckingham Palace. At one of the public demonstrations Elizabeth was arrested, and Rose, her far from suffragist companion, was also taken to prison. It was an experience to cure any enthusiasm that was only lightly rooted. When the major suffrage campaign was carried out in 1912, Elizabeth was no longer interested. Her marriage to Lawrence Kirbridge had broken up, she had had a baby by another man and an affair with a Jewish financier, and she had married again, this time to an American lawyer with whom she had gone to live in New York.

The year 1909 had been a memorable one all in all, but for reasons that were not then apparent, it would certainly remain in the memories of the Bellamys, their staff, and their guests as the Year the King Came to Dinner.

Richard Bellamy and Lady Marjorie were of the wrong generation and type to belong to the King's set. But they had been royal guests in their time, and Lady Marjorie was beautiful and known to possess great charm and tact. Inevitably, they took their place in the rota of those who would be honoured by being

Cells occupied by the suffragettes in Holloway Prison

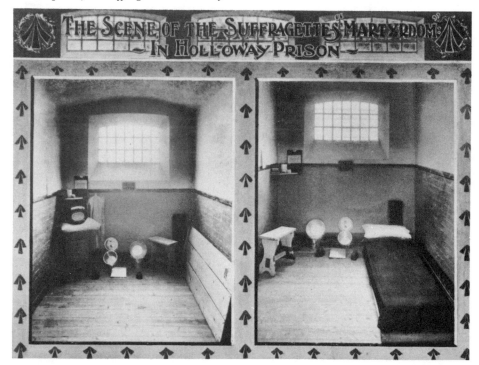

allowed to entertain the King. It was no light obligation. Edward might or might not be the arch-vulgarian Henry James had dubbed him, but he liked his food to the point of gluttony, and his figure bore adequate testimony to the fact. Mrs. Bridges's skill and ingenuity were, however, equal to any occasion. She produced a menu that did not extend to the twelve courses sometimes served for the King's delectation but that was without doubt ample enough to satisfy even him. This was her planned dinner:

Caviare

Royal Natives

Consommé de Volaille

Saumon d'Écosse, Sauce Médoc

Paté de Perdrix

Selle d'Agneau de Lait Persillé

Pommes Frou Frou

Petits Pois de Nice à la menthe

Sorbet au Champagne

Cigarettes Russes (these were permitted to ladies daring enough to smoke in public)

Pintadeau Rôti

Salade coeurs de Laitue

Asperges, Sauce Hollandaise

Gateau

Buissons d'Écrevisses

Fruits

The dishes were, of course, silver, the family silver used only on special occasions. They tended, a young Edwardian guest noticed, to make the food rather cold, but their use was absolutely *de rigueur*. The table, when fully laid, made a wonderful picture. Though the room was lit by electricity, candles glowed in elaborate silver candelabra with discreet silk shades, and silver epergnes held exotic flower arrangements from which ivy trailed, encircling the table decorations. Silver card-holders informed each guest where he or she should sit (except at the King's place, left unmarked). Five glasses, for different wines, including the Moet et Chandon Dry Imperial champagne (1900), sat by each place setting, and the damask napkins were folded into the shape of bishops' mitres, except for that at the head of the table, which simulated a fan.

The rules of conduct at such a dinner party were endless. Firstly, there would be no standing about for anything up to an hour drinking aperitifs. Although the great chef of the Reform Club, Alexis Soyer, had opened the first cocktail bar in England as long ago as 1851, the cocktail habit had not yet caught on in high society. With such a number of excellent wines, who needed an aperitif? "Sherry is but little drunk at dinner parties," said the manuals of polite behaviour.

Every lady guest knew that when she had taken her seat she must at once remove her gloves and unfold her napkin. Her soup must be "eaten" with a tablespoon, not drunk, and in Lady Marjorie's house the fish would be eaten with two silver forks. A knife and fork would be used for the asparagus and the salad and a fork with the sweets. The principle was that one used the instrument likely to convey the least possible quantity from the plate to one's mouth, in token of a sublime disregard for hunger. Only the poor or the greedy spooned their food up in disgusting amounts.

The service was swift and silent. A hired waiter had been called in to assist, for the King objected to female servants waiting at table. The conversation had to be neatly balanced, each person conversing equally with the one on either side of him or her. If the King became bored the symptoms would be quickly perceived by Mrs. Keppel, his current mistress, seated opposite him, and she would swiftly and tactfully intervene in the conversation. It was an understood thing that Mrs. Keppel should be asked with His Majesty. A strange, unspoken "understanding" prevailed at his court, by which Queen Alexandra graciously received and even entertained ladies who she knew perfectly well to be her husband's lights of love; but it was equally understood that on informal occasions the King and Mrs. Keppel would be asked together, the Queen being otherwise occupied. A public humiliation was more than even her wise and tolerant nature could be expected to bear.

The days of the numerous mistresses, even of Mrs. Langtry, the "Jersey Lily," were over. In these his last years the King had become what might be termed doubly monogamous—faithful only to his wife, on the one hand, and to George Keppel's wife on the other.

Nobody at the Bellamys' table would be unschooled in the ways of dining out. For those entering society for the first time, at less important tables than this one, there were innumerable, frightening traps. *Lady's Realm* warned:

115

Mr. Hudson directs the setting of the table for the King's visit.

(OVERLEAF) *The table set and the meal prepared, the Bellamys entertain the King and Mrs. Keppel.*

Mrs. George Keppel

"Don't spread your knife and fork across your plate when you have finished eating with them.

"Don't make a point of finishing the last mouthful on your plate, or the last piece of bread.

"The wineglass is never drained at a draught in polite society; nor is it considered polite to eat very quickly . . . scraping the edge of the knife against the plate is unpardonable. It produces a grating noise that is excessively unpleasant.

"In dealing with the bread, use neither knife nor fork. It must be broken with the fingers. (There is a story of an absent-minded and shortsighted prelate who, with the remark 'My bread, I think?' dug his fork into the white hand of a lady who sat beside him.)

"It requires some expertness and practice for a man with a moustache to take soup in a perfectly inoffensive manner . . . the well-bred young man manages better than this. He eats in small morsels and absolutely without sound of any kind."

With so many opportunities for making hideous social gaffes it was a wonder that Edwardian dinner parties went off so smoothly, particularly when royalty was present to make everyone that much more nervous. But they had all been trained rigidly from the nursery by nannies who would stand no nonsense or bad manners, and they acquitted themselves beautifully. After the King's departure a monumental clearing-up remained to be done at the Bellamys. Ruby, the new scullery maid from Yorkshire, was responsible for dealing with the mountains of dirty plates, glasses, and cutlery, which had to be washed by hand, dried, and put away before the staff could retire to bed. But for the King, returning in comfort to Buckingham Palace, there awaited a pleasant nightcap of whisky or liqueur brandy. He looked back on a pleasant, normal dinner party. He hoped to enjoy many more.

The belowstairs view of entertaining

The new King, the Prince of Wales, Prince Albert, the Kaiser, and the Kings of Spain and Bulgaria pass in homage to Edward VII before Victoria's statue at Windsor.

CHAPTER SEVEN

Now Thank We All Our God

But the Bellamys had entertained their King for the last time. Overweight was catching up with him after decades of self-indulgence. On his usual spring visit to Biarritz he suffered from bronchial trouble, but rallied and came back to London apparently restored to health.

The recovery was brief. Early in May the complacency of London was shattered by the news that the King had had a relapse and was seriously ill. The Archbishop of Canterbury had been sent for; the royal family was on its way to the bedside. With wonderful generosity, Queen Alexandra summoned Alice Keppel to the palace. She knew that her husband, unfaithful so many times, would wish to see his last and most cherished mistress before he died. When the end came, Alice had gone, and his wife was there by his side, with their two daughters, Louise and Toria, their son Prince George and his wife, May; for once Kaiser Wilhelm had not managed to capture any limelight by a dramatic dash to the scene.

For four days the dead King's catafalque remained in Westminster Hall, a place of pilgrimage for mourning crowds; then came the state funeral at Windsor. He was to lie beneath the stones of St. George's Chapel, not in the mausoleum at Frogmore, nearby, where Queen Victoria and the Prince Consort lay sculptured in marble. Even in death his parents were not anxious for his company.

Now the Bellamys, their staff, and the rest of Great Britain's inhabitants were Georgians, not Edwardians. It was a startling change. The reign had been so

The new Queen, Mary: the epitome of Georgian staidness and sobriety

short—only nine years—and the last King George had died in 1830. The new monarch was a sharp contrast to his father. Shortish but without his father's stockiness, bearded, and diffident of bearing, he lacked the imperious manners of his forebears. Court dress and decorations did not suit him; he looked better in the naval uniform he had worn so frequently in his role of "Sailor Prince." His taller, stouter wife, now no longer Princess May but Queen Mary, matched him in staidness. Not for them the dancing, gambling, theatregoing life of Edward's court. Edward himself had once remarked that "there were a very good country squire and his wife lost in George and May." The new King liked best to be at Sandringham (where the Queen Dowager took up her residence), managing his estates, riding, shooting, and fishing in a very much more private manner than his father. Queen Mary was a devoted, if not sentimental, mother to her children. What characterized the pair, people said, was their strict sense of duty.

It had been their sense of duty that had made them man and wife. Princess May had been engaged to the Duke of Clarence, "Eddy" of somewhat less than blessed memory (detective historians half a century later would speculate on the vague possibility of his having been Jack the Ripper). On Eddy's early death in 1891 Princess May had been swiftly passed on to his younger brother, George. Fortunately they suited each other, and they were good for England. May had suffered in youth from cheerfully improvident parents and had in consequence developed a sharp eye for household economies and for a bargain of any kind, especially in the field of antiques, of which she was a knowledgeable collector. She had little tolerance for people who overstepped the mark morally. A lady who had been readily accepted at the court of King Edward might be dismayed to find her name no longer on the list of those received at that of King George. In one such case, as reported by *Strand* magazine, an official of the Lord Chamberlain's department pointed out to the King that one such lady might well be restored to favour.

"Her Majesty has removed the name," said His Majesty coldly, "and that is quite sufficient for me. Personally, I know nothing of the lady, but that is neither here nor there. She cannot be present in view of the Queen's decision."

The Prince of Wales, now sixteen, had been christened Edward Albert Christian George Andrew Patrick David, but in the family he was given only the last name. He was a slender, fragile-looking, almost lady-faced boy, with a shy manner and a charming smile, much beloved of the people. He was

David, Prince of Wales: "a shy manner and a charming smile"

frequently brought to public notice in one capacity or another and in costumes ranging from the robes of the Garter to the Highland garb that suited him a fraction better than it did his father or his brothers, George, Albert, and Henry. At present he was serving as a naval cadet, regardless of any like or dislike on his part for the life of the sea.

"That child looks put upon," said Lady Marjorie when at a royal garden party she had made her curtsey to Queen Mary and had received a shy smile from the blushing Prince. "They expect too much of him."

It was a more prophetic judgement than she knew.

The only girl in the royal family, Princess Mary, was also shy and retiring, educated in the palace schoolroom with little contact with her own contemporaries. The fourth and youngest brother, Prince John, was seldom seen by the public; he was mentally retarded and destined for an early death.

On the eve of King Edward's funeral a phenomenon occurred: Halley's Comet, not seen since 1835, blazed across the skies. It was a portent of something, people said—but of what? Certainly the times were changing rapidly and not only in royal circles. Britain itself could no longer be secure in its island fastness. The year before, Louis Blériot had flown the Channel, and in 1910 popular imagination was caught by the spectacular flight by C. S. Rolls to France and back in 90 minutes. People still rushed out to look up when an aeroplane made its way overhead, but it had become more commonplace for a pilot and two passengers to whirl along two miles above the earth, and news came to Richard and his colleagues that aerial wireless telegraphy was being tested out in France.

The wireless certainly worked on ships. In January 1910 the music-hall performer known as Belle Elmore, wife of Dr. Hawley Harvey Crippen, disappeared from their house in North London. Her husband explained that she had run away to America and later gave out that she had died there. When suspicion grew (caused partly by the presence in the house of an attractive young secretary, Ethel Le Neve, who was seen to be wearing some of Mrs. Crippen's jewellery), Crippen disappeared, taking Ethel with him. Some time later, after grisly human remains had been found buried in the cellar, Inspector Dew of Scotland Yard began to take a great interest in the whereabouts of the missing two. On the Canadian Pacific liner *Montrose* the keen eyes of Captain Kendall took note of certain curious things about the relationship of a Mr. Robinson and his very girlish "son." He sent a wireless message to Liverpool, to which

Inspector Dew replied that he would follow the *Montrose* in a faster ship and board her in the St. Lawrence River.

The scheme worked. Disguised as a pilot, he was introduced to "Mr. Robinson" by Captain Kendall and immediately revealed his identity.

"Thank God," said the mousy, shortsighted little man. "Thank God it's over. The suspense has been too great. I couldn't stand it any longer."

The first arrest through the assistance of wireless telegraphy had been made. In November Crippen was hanged for the murder of his wife. Ethel Le Neve was acquitted.

Early in January 1911 the British public was entertained by another dramatic story. Civil violence was then rare enough to make what became known as the

Siege of Sidney Street a sensation. A group of anarchists had killed three policemen while shooting their way out of a house in Houndsditch, in London's East End. Clues led the police to another house, in Stepney, where a criminal leader known as Peter the Painter was lying hidden with two of his gang. The house was surrounded and shots fired. The police came off worst, and the Home Secretary was informed that there was a serious situation to be tackled. He arrived in person to take charge of the massive siege operation, very correctly dressed in a fur coat (the day was cold) and a shining top hat, his chubby face alight with the joy of battle. He was Winston Churchill, aged thirty-seven, the brilliant young politician who had been in turn soldier, war correspondent in South Africa, Conservative, and Liberal. Later in the year he would be made First Lord of the Admiralty.

Winston Churchill in command at a comic-opera "battle"

The Rolls-Royce Silver Ghost

Although the Sidney Street Siege fizzled out, as did the flames engulfing the house, in the jets from firemen's hoses, it had been orchestrated into a massively heroic affair, involving 750 police and a detachment of the Scots Guards. The grand manner belonged naturally to Winston Churchill.

Just before the turn of the year Richard Bellamy had disposed of the Renault and bought a Silver Ghost from the Rolls-Royce firm. In time to come it would be the treasured, expensive toy of a veteran-car collector, restored, polished, and groomed with loving pride, and copied, like its contemporaries, in millions of tiny plastic models that small boys could assemble for themselves. In its own time it was regarded with less reverence. The comic papers showed children playing on railway lines because the roads were no longer safe playgrounds. Many early photographs demonstrate that they had formerly played in the middle of roads and streets in both town and country, completely safe unless a horse should bolt and scatter them. As for the horse itself, a *Punch* strip cartoon of 1910 portrayed a weeping horse being driven to the Motor Show in a motor van inscribed "No further use for him"; in the final picture the van has broken down and the triumphant horse is pulling it. But the motorcar had come to stay, as Thomas Watkins, the Bellamys' chauffeur, realized when he managed to secure himself a small motor business in Kilburn, West London, and became independent.

   A tragic, heroic piece of history was made in 1911, far from Belgravia and the doings of early Georgian society. Robert Falcon Scott, who had been a naval officer and had already led an Antarctic expedition in his ship *Discovery* in 1904,

Piccadilly Circus, 1910, with the inevitable road mending in progress

Anticlimax instead of triumph: The faces of Scott and his companions betray their bitter disappointment.

organized another one in 1910 in a bid to be the first man to reach the South Pole. With Edward Wilson, Edgar Evans, Lawrence Oates, and H. R. Bowers, he set out in the *Terra Nova* on his quest, beginning the last stage of the journey in November 1911. On January 18, 1912, the five reached the Pole—only to find that the Norwegian explorer Amundsen had planted his flag there a month earlier. Bitterly disappointed, harassed by frostbite, scurvy, and hunger, Scott and his party set out on a return journey that was to end in starvation and a dreadful death on the Antarctic ice.

But though both Upstairs and Downstairs read such news with sadness (and Richard Bellamy frowned over reports of strikes among dockers, railwaymen, and weavers and took part in stormy scenes in the House over the Parliament Bill, which sharply divided the Liberals and the Tory diehards), there was plenty of light relief. The Coronation Summer of 1911 was hot. Londoners rejoiced, danced, and got drunk in dusty streets and parks where the grass had withered in the sizzling temperatures. Theatregoers were humming the unforgettable tunes of Oscar Straus's *Waltz Dream* and Franz Lehar's *The Count of Luxembourg*, and at His Majesty's Theatre in London's Haymarket a great Gala Performance was given to celebrate the Coronation. The proceeds—a handsome £4,628—were donated to a pension fund for aged actors and actresses. The ageing but still beautiful Ellen Terry was touring England with her unique Shakespearean recitals, bringing Shakespeare's women to life in a series of vivid "lectures" that drew crowded houses. She had once told Henry Irving that Shakespeare was the only man she had ever really loved, and for the past year she had been conveying that love and her profound understanding of the dramatist to American audiences before bringing them home to England.

Ellen Terry: ". . . ageing but still beautiful"

131

"Then there was the Russian ballet . . ."

Then there was the Russian ballet—Diaghilev's company appearing for the first time in London (but it would be 1913 before they really took the city by storm, with the splendours of Nijinsky's dancing, Stravinsky's music, and Bakst's blazing colors). The ballerina Anna Pavlova was dancing her famous role in *The Death of the Swan* at the Palace Theatre; she would continue to dance it over and over again to the end of her life. On a much humbler and more national level, England was discovering her own forgotten art of the dance, with the foundation by Cecil Sharp of the English Folk-Dance Society. Young and not so young men and women would gather in their free time, dressed in their idea of the country-folk dress in past ages, to dance to the simple music of accordions or fiddles the tunes that had for centuries been heard on village greens or at the Harvest Home festivities: "Gathering Peascods," the "Handkerchief Dance,"

"Blow Away the Morning Dew," and many others collected by Sharp and his fellow enthusiasts (in not a few cases with the words "cleaned up").

About this time Richard Bellamy, who was writing a biography of his late father-in-law Lord Southwold, engaged a lady secretary, Hazel Forrest. No longer were such young women referred to by the name of their machines, as "typewriters." A domestic handbook of 1911 declared: "Years ago the woman in business was an unknown quantity; today she is an accepted fact. There is scarcely a business career nowadays which cannot be entered by a clever woman, and from the typist at £1 a week to the manageress or the proprietress of large commercial enterprises we find women working side by side with men . . . there is still, however, a deplorable tendency to make women work longer and at lesser salaries than men in the mere clerical positions."

Richard Bellamy and his new secretary, Hazel Forrest

The would-be typist was recommended to spend a year or two training for her work at one of the many business colleges, such as the one founded by Sir Isaac Pitman. She was advised, in applying for a post, that "an employer does not want to know how difficult you find it to get work, or if you are an orphan, or if your mother is an invalid." But such would be the case of most of the young women who needed work. Those of Elizabeth Bellamy's caste would not think of taking a job for the sake of working. It was the Hazels, the genteel young persons, highly respectable but not quite ladies, who would offer their services to large business firms and private employers. Many stories in popular magazines dealt with them, their worthiness and struggles, and their ultimate romances that released them from the necessity of a rather wearing job that required, in Hazel's case, carrying her own typewriter about with her. It was only natural that such a young person should live in Wimbledon, in the "suburbia" still looked down upon, though Wimbledon was in fact already the world-renowned home of lawn tennis and had been so since 1874, when the ancient game had been revived in an effort to help the exchequer of the All England Croquet Club. In the same year it seems to have been introduced to the United States, whose players would share first-class honours with the English for many years.

Hazel did not feel particularly happy or unhappy at 165 Eaton Place. The Bellamys were cool, considerate employers. James, now working for a tea-shipping company and amusing himself with the latest music from America played on his gramophone, was as yet no problem to her. Elizabeth was married and gone to America. Lady Marjorie was soon to travel, also westwards on the *Titanic*, with her brother and his wife, to stay on their new ranch in Calgary, Canada. She was longing to see Elizabeth's daughter Lucy, who had been only a baby when Elizabeth had married her lawyer. An advance present had been sent to Lucy, a parcel of Beatrix Potter's nursery books and the fantasy *The Wind in the Willows*.

Not merely the Bellamy household but the world was shaken to its foundations by the news that came one April day in 1912. The White Star liner *Titanic* had struck an iceberg and had sunk with terrible loss of life.

She had been built in a spirit of keen competition. The Cunard and White Star lines had for years been trying to outbuild each other, to produce bigger, better, more luxurious liners, floating hotels in which the rich of both sides of the Atlantic might cross to each other's shores surrounded by every imaginable

The Titanic *before the disaster*

comfort. American money put up by Pierpont Morgan financed the *Titanic*. She was larger than her predecessor the *Olympic*, she had more first-class accommodation than any previous ship, and even the immigrant passengers were better provided for than earlier ones had been. The only flaw in this so-called unsinkable monster was that nobody had taken the trouble to find out whether she *was* unsinkable; and evidence points to her being quite otherwise. Her sixteen watertight compartments had been badly placed in order to make room for extra passenger accommodation, so that the underwater iceberg projection tore into them like a dagger, letting in the floods of water that sank her in less than three hours. Through some strange oversight there had been no boat drill. When the alarm was given, nobody quite knew what to do, and the handling of the lifeboats seems to have been utterly mismanaged. About 1,500 people died in the disaster, and but for the gallant rescue dash of the small Cunarder *Carpathia* many others would have gone down with them.

Lady Marjorie was dead, but life in the Bellamy household must go on. In time Richard was even able to contemplate remarriage, but the lady, Countess

First news of the tragedy

Lili de Vernay, was emphatically not suitable. Beautiful, amoral, an unashamed fortune hunter, she belonged to the Vienna that was still the city of song, operetta, and romance, the last bastion of the dying Austrian Empire. The Imperial double-headed eagle was losing its feathers, would soon be finished, like those game birds at which tired old Emperor Franz Josef still potted away at his shooting lodge in the Tyrol. The year 1913 saw uneasy stirrings everywhere. Late in 1912 a three-cornered Presidential contest had seen Woodrow Wilson triumph over the Progressive Roosevelt and the Republican Taft. "Men's hearts wait upon us, men's lives hang in the balance, men's hopes call upon us to say what we will do," he said. It was, indeed, a time to gather strength. War raged in the Balkans, the Queen Dowager's brother, King George of Greece, was assassinated. Germany, Austria, and France were spending enormous sums on arms and military equipment.

Yet the readers of *Strand* magazine, engaged in a whimsical little contest to decide who were the ten greatest men then alive and the most likely to have statues erected to them in the future, selected (among a curious collection of names including Kipling, Thomas Hardy, and Theodore Roosevelt), in eight out of thirteen lists, Kaiser Wilhelm II. Meanwhile, in June 1913 he was celebrating in Berlin the twenty-fifth anniversary of his accession. Among the many deputations was one from fifty-four peace societies of America, led by Mr. Carnegie, who brought a "magnificent illuminated address" and, thanking the Kaiser for twenty-five years of peace, remarked, "You are the best ally we have in your great country." In the courtyard of the royal castle schoolchildren marched and sang old chorales, while the massed bands of the Guards played "Now Thank We All Our God."

In August the Palace of Peace was opened at The Hague, Holland, "a milestone marking the advance of the reign of reason in the promotion of harmonious international relationships." Mr. Hudson read, with raised eyebrows, of its opening.

NATIONAL HEALTH INSURANCE

Name of Member *Ernest Eady* No. **23**

Full rate of Sickness Benefit...*10*...s....*0*....d. a week.

TABLE A. REDUCED RATES OF BENEFIT.   5

Number of Net Penalty Arrears.	ORDINARY RATE OF BENEFIT.										
	s. d. 10 0	s. d. 9 6	s. d. 9 0	s. d. 8 6	s. d. 8 0	s. d. 7 6	s. d. 7 0	s. d. 6 6	s. d. 6 0	s. d. 5 6	s. d. 5 0
1	9 5	8 11	8 5	7 11	7 5	6 11	6 5	5 11	5 5	4 11	4 5
2	8 10	8 4	7 10	7 4	6 10	6 4	5 10	5 4	4 10	4 4	3 10
3	8 3	7 9	7 3	6 9	6 3	5 9	5 3	4 9	4 3	3 9	3 3
4	7 8	7 2	6 8	6 2	5 8	5 2	4 8	4 2	3 8	3 2	2 8
5	7 1	6 7	6 1	5 7	5 1	4 7	4 1	3 7	3 1	2 7	2 1
6	6 6	6 0	5 6	5 0	4 6	4 0	3 6	3 0	2 6	2 0	2 0
7	5 11	5 5	4 11	4 5	3 11	3 5	2 11	2 5	2 0	2 0	2 0
8	5 4	4 10	4 4	3 10	3 4	2 10	2 4	2 0	2 0	2 0	2 0
9	4 9	4 3	3 9	3 3	2 9	2 3	2 0	2 0	2 0	2 0	2 0
10	4 2	3 8	3 2	2 8	2 2	2 0	2 0	2 0	2 0	2 0	2 0
11	3 7	3 1	2 7	2 1	2 0	2 0	2 0	2 0	2 0	2 0	2 0
12	3 0	2 6	2 0	2 0	2 0	2 0	2 0	2 0	2 0	2 0	2 0
13	2 5	2 0	2 0	2 0	2 0	2 0	2 0	2 0	2 0	2 0	2 0
14	2 0	2 0	2 0	2 0	2 0	2 0	2 0	2 0	2 0	2 0	2 0
15	2 0	2 0	2 0	2 0	2 0	2 0	2 0	2 0	2 0	2 0	2 0
16	2 0	2 0	2 0	2 0	2 0	2 0	2 0	2 0	2 0	2 0	2 0

TABLE B. RESERVE CONTRIBUTIONS.

To be credited at July, 1914.		To be credited at the end of each subsequent Contribution Year.	
Date of Entry into Insurance.	Number of Reserve Contributions.	Date of Entry into Insurance.	Number of Reserve Contributions.
Not later than 21st July, 1912 ...	6	Before commencement of Contribution Year	3
After 21st July, 1912, but not later than 12th January, 1913 ...	5	During first half of Contribution Year...	2
After 12th January, 1913, but not later than 13th July, 1913 ...	4	During second half of Contribution Year...	1
After 13th July, 1913, but not later than 11th January, 1914 ...	2		
After 11th January, 1914, but not later than 5th July, 1914 ...	1		

One of the first National Health Insurance books

CHAPTER EIGHT

August Bank Holiday: 1914

Even Mr. Hudson, with his notably pessimistic outlook, could not have anticipated what the year 1914 would come to mean to him, his fellow servants, and his employers.

Certainly there were troubles. the Irish Home Rule squabble; the crisis of the suffragette campaign, in which a woman slashed the Rokeby Venus in the National Gallery with a chopper; another lay in wait for Asquith and Churchill in the House of Commons lobby, armed with a riding whip; and all over the country fires were started and bombs exploded, one going off under the seat of the Coronation Chair in Westminster Abbey. But there was nothing to indicate that these troubles were the forerunners of things unimaginably worse. The year 1914 began calmly enough at No. 165, after the excitement when Georgina Worsley, Richard Bellamy's young ward, had stolen food from Mrs. Bridges's larder to take to the new maid Daisy's wretchedly poor family. The New Year bells had rung out as usual. All over the country parlour baritones would be singing to their port-enlivened families that

> . . . 'twas a night that should banish all sin,
> For the bells were ringing the Old Year out,
> And the New Year in.

139

It would be the last year of England as she had so long been; the world would never be the same again.

Looking at it squarely, Mrs. Bridges said to Mr. Hudson, they were better off than they'd ever been. At first they had resented the passing of the National Insurance Act, which had taken 4d a week from them in return for a stamp on their Insurance Card. But it meant that they were now entitled to free medical treatment, sick pay for a number of weeks, and, if they were unlucky enough to contract pulmonary tuberculosis, which killed off so many, they would get special consideration. "And this Old Age Pension—well, there was a lot of talk about how it was going to turn us into a lot of drunks and squanderers when we was turned seventy. But that won't happen to us, not likely. And when we're too old for service we shan't starve. Likewise, if Edward or one of the young ones got sacked, there's these new Labour Exchanges he could go to," said Mrs. Bridges.

The maids—Rose, Daisy, and even Ruby—thought that 1914 fashions were very flattering and sensible. For the female silhouette, which had been all sorts of tortured shapes in its time, had returned to something resembling nature. The painful corset and the tight bust-bodice had been replaced by a garment invented by a Frenchman, Paul Poiret—the brassiere. Whatever Queen Mary was wearing to create her extraordinary figure, her female subjects snatched at this new freedom and the gentler appearance it gave them. There were more drastic changes. Ankles appeared, even a glimpse of calves for the very daring. The high-boned collar had gone; blouses tended to be collarless or to have the round "Peter Pan" collar. *The Times* was rather severe upon some of these innovations:

> *Never before have women dared to show their legs as they have shown the during the last year or so . . . . never before have they shown such masculine tendencies about the nether limbs. . . . The tailor-made of this season is so absolutely unlike any kind of skirt that women have ever worn before, and the silhouette it gives is so very different from any other that we have seen among feminine fashions that we naturally wonder from what source the designers draw their inspiration. They have gone, it seems, to old pictures of men, not women. . . .*

Millinery, commented *The Times*, was also governed by men's fashions: "the boyish silhouette demands a raking toque and a jaunty feather." The raking toques were clumsy, top-heavy hats heavily trimmed, sometimes with ribbon or

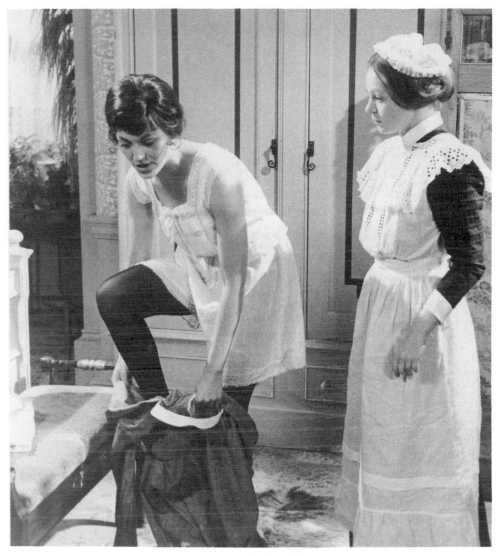

Georgina dressing: ". . . lingerie prettier than it had ever been"

artificial fruit and flowers but all too often with the feathers of exotic birds, ospreys, birds of paradise, lyre birds, all wantonly shot to provide millinery decoration. For half a century *Punch* had been protesting against this cruelty, but still it went on. For those who, like the Downstairs servants, would not be able to afford such luxury, there were the feathers—sometimes whole wings— of English wild birds, the seagull, the lark, the blackbird. They thought nothing of it.

For the rich girl, such as Georgina, there were gorgeous clothes inspired by the ballet—the "Oriental look" Bakst and Diaghilev had brought to England: vivid colours, gold and silver embroidery, jewelled shoulder straps, sometimes, for evening occasions, harem trousers worn with a tunic. Underneath they would wear lingerie prettier than it had ever been—"indecent things of cobweb thickness" trimmed with lace, satin bows, threaded ribbon, and embroidery. A simple "princess slip" that was an all-in-one undergarment replaced the cumbersome layers of petticoats of the past; panties of nainsook, delectably edged with ribbon; and, of course, silk stockings and shoes that had to match the dress because they were now visible. It was as though the unsuccessful March of the Women had terminated in an enormous fashion parade.

As for the men, they remained as they had been more or less since the early days of Queen Victoria, sober rooks in blacks and greys, sweating in tight collars, uncomfortable in waistcoats and long badly fitting trousers.

There was plenty doing in the world of entertainment. In the past it had been a rare treat for Edward and Daisy to slip out to the bioscope to see a moving picture. These little "bijou" cinemas were often small halls or converted shops, seldom holding more than 300, and going by such names as the De Luxe, the Gem, the Élite. By 1914 these cosy places had given way to "picture palaces," larger, showier, more comfortable than their predecessors. A lady pianist thumped out "struggle music" for fights, languorously strummed tearjerking melodies for partings and death scenes, worked up the audience's excitement with appropriate strains as Pearl White endured *The Perils of Pauline*, which, said the handout for the serial, "includes flying machine accidents, thrilling rescues, fires at sea, train wrecks, automobile accidents, in fact, everything that can be introduced as a thrill."

Unlike later performers, these intrepid players did not hand over to the stunt man when the plot required them to do something dangerous. "Sensationalism today is the rage, and grave risks are incurred to satisfy this demand," said a *Strand* writer of early 1914, describing the awful flirtations with death of Babs Neville (stunned in a barge fight and half drowned in the Thames), Blanche Sweet (transferred from the back of one "madly galloping" horse to another), and Mary Fuller (obliged to escape from a seventh-floor window by sliding down a rope made of bedclothes).

All films were not sensational; there were concessions to the classics. Film versions were made of Dickens' *A Christmas Carol* and *The Chimes*, of novels by

The intrepid Pearl White

"Mr. Charlie Chaplin—himself!"

popular authors such as Hall Caine and Rider Haggard, and even of the poems of Tennyson, which must have made remarkable viewing. Humour was becoming more sophisticated: little Charlie Chaplin was for the first time seen on the screens of Britain in *Making a Living*, one of the Keystone Comedies. He had graduated from the music hall and stage, as had many other film players, including such theatrical luminaries as Ellen Terry, Johnston Forbes-

Robertson, Lewis Waller, Sir John Hare, and Irene Vanbrugh. But others came to the fore without being previously known to the theatre public.

In the London theatres 1914 was a bumper year. Oscar Asche and Lily Brayton were starring in *Kismet* at the Glove, and at the New, Cyril Maude was spending infinite time and trouble in making up nightly as the eighty-three-year-old character Grumpy. Gerald du Maurier could be seen in *An Ideal Husband*, and Mrs. Pat Campbell was playing Eliza to Sir Herbert Tree's Higgins in Shaw's *Pygmalion*. If opera were to one's taste, there was a feast of gorgeous productions in the Sir Thomas Beecham season at Drury Lane, with Chaliapin singing *Boris Godunov*.

For those who liked more active amusements, there was the institution known as the *thé dansant*, which was exactly what it sounded like—tea, cakes, dancing, and flirtation to the music of a modest little orchestra. Rose's Australian friend Gregory took her to one; it was a good opportunity to further their acquaintanceship in intimate, lightly romantic surroundings. *Thés dansants* were very popular with spinsters and widows on the lookout for a partner who might turn into a husband. But Rose and Gregory were unlikely ever to perform the new, scandalous tango. The actress Phyllis Dare gave it her blessing in an article called "Tips for the Tango." "Please don't imagine that there is the slightest impropriety about any single movement of the tango as it is danced today. It has long since been rescued from the cabarets of the Argentine and of Montmartre." But others were horrified by the intimacy of the thing—dancing face to face, practically cheek to cheek—it was shocking. Father Bernard Vaughan in particular denounced it as one of those "animal dances that have no *raison d'être* but to gratify animal passions." Young people like James and Georgina were undeterred. They did the tango, the maxixe, the chicken reel, turkey trot, and bunny hug, and they felt they belonged to the Age of Ragtime.

England had unusually fine dry weather that summer of 1914. Mr. Hudson was often at Lord's and the Oval, for though there was no Test series (the M.C.C. team was in South Africa, among them Jack Hobbs, Wilfred Rhodes, and Frank Woolley) there were plenty of county cricket matches. The County Championship would not, however, be played out that year for pressing reasons: the Oval ground was commandeered by the military in August. It had been a remarkable year for sporting events. There had been the unique occasion at Twickenham, with the attendance of King George at a Rugby Union Match

Mr. Gerald du Maurier and Mr. Laurence Irving in Raffles

Miss Lily Brayton in Kismet

Derby Day at Epsom: a remarkable entourage

between England and Ireland. He was the first English monarch to watch an international match. He also honoured a baseball game on the Chelsea ground, Chicago White Sox versus the New York Giants, and the Cup Final at the Crystal Palace. It is difficult to imagine either Edward VII or Queen Victoria sitting through such sporting events.

When Grand National time came round Mr. Hudson had a small flutter on the King's horse, Twelfth Lancer, but was disappointed to read that the winner had been a rank outsider, Sunloch. With a Scottish-sounding name like that he felt he should have had the sense to back it.

Derby time in May brought a certain amount of apprehension. The previous year had been marked by tragedy when an extremist suffragette, Emily Davidson, had thrown herself over the rails in front of the King's horse and had been fatally injured, though both jockey and horse survived. This year three rows of rails had been put up at Tattenham Corner, and over 3,000 policemen and C.I.D. men were in attendance. But there were no more martyrs.

Nobody at No. 165 followed boxing. In polite circles it was considered a rough sport, brutal and degrading, and Mrs. Bridges was shocked to hear that there had actually been women spectators, a thousand of them, at the Bombardier Wells–Colin Bell fight and twice as many at a lightweight championship match. Whatever were things coming to? she wondered. She was not aware that a youngish theatre manager, Charles B. Cochran, with a flair for promoting entertainment of all kinds, had decided to make boxing respectable and would

Wells vs. Carpentier: His seconds chair the winner to his corner.

succeed, as he did with most things he touched. He watched with keen interest the fight between Britain's "Gunboat" Smith and France's young Georges Carpentier for the title of "light, white, heavyweight champion of the world." But the result was disappointing, Smith being disqualified for a blow to the head and Carpentier taking the title of world champion amid squabbles.

Henley Regatta took place in a sizzling heat wave. Temperatures were still up in the 80s and 90s when the staff of No. 165 went on their August Bank Holiday outing to Herne Bay in Kent. Hazel and James Bellamy, who had been married now for two years, had gone to Goodwood at the end of July for the Cup race, but Richard did not accompany them, having other things on his mind. There was serious concern at Westminster about the situation abroad. On June 28 the Archduke Franz Ferdinand, heir to the throne of Austria-Hungary, had been assassinated by Serbians with his wife at Sarajevo in Bosnia. Austria had first sent a note to Serbia, demanding immense concessions and blaming Serbia for the assassination. A declaration of war followed. Russia was Serbia's ally; Germany backed Austria. Should the enormous military might of Germany be called out, France, the ally of Russia, would be immediately attacked through Belgium, though Belgium herself was neutral. Should Germany march, Britain would be forced to act against her as a guarantor of Belgium's neutrality.

The public learned of the crisis through the newspapers. "To hell with Serbia!" shrieked a *John Bull* street placard. Others said, "The horrid spectre of war" and "Europe drifting to disaster." Alarm spread; some prudent people began to hoard food as prices rose. Others found it impossible to believe—even after the Germans marched into Belgium—that war could become a reality in that beautiful, blazing weather. It was a dream, something that only happened in far-off countries. Yet it was curiously exciting. The young people, Georgina, Daisy, Edward, Ruby, could hardly remember the Boer War. Even Mr. Hudson, politically informed and a natural prophet of doom, was quite unable to comprehend what a European war would be like; he, and millions of other Britons, saw it only in terms of patriotism and glory.

And so, when at midnight (11:00 P.M. British time) on August 4 London knew that Germany had failed to answer Britain's ultimatum calling upon Germany to withdraw from Belgium, hysterical excitement broke out. Outside Buckingham Palace swirling crowds sang Elgar's "Land of Hope and Glory" as the royal family appeared on the balcony. There was dancing in the street,

The ultimatum expires: the Daily Mail, *August 4, 19*

GREAT BRITAIN DECLARES WAR ON GERMANY.

SUMMARY REJECTION OF BRITISH ULTIMATUM.

ALL EYES ON THE NORTH SEA

INVASION OF BELGIUM.

The following announcement was issued at the Foreign Office at 12.15 a.m.:—

"Owing to the summary rejection by the German Government of the request made by His Majesty's Government for assurances that the neutrality of Belgium would be respected, His Majesty's Ambassador in Berlin has received his passports, and His Majesty's Government has declared to the German Government that a state of war exists between Great Britain and Germany as from 11 p.m. on August 4."

Huge crowds in Whitehall and Trafalgar Square greeted the news with round after round of cheers.

11 p.m. London time is midnight Berlin time, the hour at which the British ultimatum expired.

The King held a Council at midnight to sign the proclamation of war.

Great Britain had sent an ultimatum to Germany which expired at midnight.

This was due to Germany's refusal to leave Belgium neutral and her invasion of that country.

The German Ambassador went to 10, Downing Street at 12.10 a.m. to receive his papers. He looked a broken man.

Sir Edward Goschen, the British Ambassador in Berlin, demanded his passports.

Admiral Jellicoe is in command of the British Fleet.

The State has taken over all the British railways.

A German warship attacked the French port Bona, in Algeria.

The main centre of interest in the war has shifted suddenly from the French frontier to the North Sea.

A land battle is not to be expected till the process of mobilisation is complete—for several days. Fleets can act instantly, immediately after a declaration of war. The most powerful ships of all Navies are maintained in a perpetual condition of readiness.

The British and German Fleets now face one another in the North Sea.

The British ultimatum to Germany required a satisfactory answer as regards the neutrality of Belgium by midnight last night.

Germany had threatened to make a passage for her armies through Belgium on Monday night "by force of arms."

German troops yesterday actually entered Belgium.

Admiral Sir John R. Jellicoe, K.C.B., the Kitchener of the Navy, has assumed supreme command of the Home Fleets, and Rear-Admiral C. E. Madden, C.V.O., has been appointed his Chief of the Staff. Field-Marshal Sir John French has been reappointed Inspector-General of the Forces.

The strength of the main British and main German Fleets in the most powerful type of ships is as follows:

	Dreadnoughts.	Pre-Dreadnoughts.	Battle Cruisers.
British	19	8	4
German	13	8	4

Both Great Britain and Germany have also brought up large numbers of older and smaller ships.

The weight of metal from the heavy guns in the British main Fleet is superior by 60 per cent. to that in the German main Fleet.

This is due to the fact that the British Dreadnoughts carry 12in. and 13.5in. guns, whereas the German Dreadnoughts only carry 11in. and 12in. guns.

The British strength in modern [...] British total available is about 70 boats, and the German force is not believed to exceed 80.

The British Fleets are manned by at least 100,000 officers and men; the German Fleets by about 65,000 men.

The British Government has taken over the control of all the railways. They will be worked by a committee of general managers as one railway. The staffs will remain as before and receive orders through their own officials.

The Government is preparing a scheme to control the distribution of the country's food supplies.

£1 notes are to be put in circulation on Friday, when millions of them will be ready. Ten shilling notes will follow later.

TWO MORE BRITISH DREADNOUGHTS.

ACQUISITION FROM TURKEY.

We are officially informed that the Government have taken over the two battleships, one completed and the other shortly due for completion, which had been ordered in this country by the Turkish Government and the two destroyer leaders ordered by the Government of Chili.

The two battleships will receive the names Agincourt and Erin, and the destroyer leaders will be called Faulkner and Broke, after two famous naval officers.

The two Dreadnought battleships are:

1. The SULTAN OSMAN I. Built by Messrs. Armstrong. She is the largest battleship yet completed, being of 27,500 tons displacement. She has seven turrets, each carrying two 12in. guns. The vessel was laid down to the order of the Brazilian Government, but was taken over by Turkey for £2,723,000.

2. The RESHADIEH.—Built by Messrs. Vickers. Displacement 23,000 tons. She has ten 13.5in. guns mounted on twin turrets on the centre line as in the King George class.

SELLING THE SKIN.

From Our Parliamentary Correspondent

I hear that on Thursday the German Ambassador in London made, on behalf of the German Government, a verbal communication to Sir Edward Grey to the effect that, in the event of Great Britain remaining neutral in Germany's war with France, Germany would undertake, "when she had brought France to her knees," not to deprive France of any of her territory in Europe but to "content herself" with taking the French Colonial possessions.

HOLLAND'S FEARS.

[...] Correspondent.

HOME FLEETS.

SUPREME COMMAND.

SIR JOHN JELLICOE, K.C.B.

THE KING'S MESSAGE TO THE FLEET.

With the approval of the King, Admiral Sir John R. Jellicoe, K.C.B., K.C.V.O., has assumed supreme command of the Home Fleets, with the acting rank of Admiral; and

Rear-Admiral Charles E. Madden, C.V.O,

ADMIRAL SIR JOHN R. JELLICOE.

has been appointed to be his Chief of the Staff.

Both appointments date from yesterday.

The King has sent the following message to Admiral Sir John Jellicoe:—

At this grave moment in our national history I send to you, and through you to the officers and men of the fleets of which you have assumed command, the assurance of my confidence that under your direction they will revive and renew the old glories of the Royal Navy and prove once again the sure shield of Britain and of her Empire in the hour of trial.

GEORGE R.I.

The King's message has been communicated to the senior naval officers on all stations outside of home waters.

SIR JOHN FRENCH.

INSPECTOR-GENERAL OF THE FORCES AGAIN.

Field-Marshal Sir John French has been appointed Inspector-General of the Forces. The appointment, which dates from August 1, was announced in the *London Gazette* last night.

This office is the one Sir John French held from 1907 until 1911, when he relieved Sir William Nicholson in the office of Chief of the Imperial General Staff. He resigned the latter appointment as the result of the repudiated guarantee to General Gough in connection with the plot against Ulster.

HUGE GERMAN CREDIT.

£250,000,000 FOR WAR.

BERLIN, Tuesday.

A Bill was presented in the Reichstag to-day authorising the Imperial Chancellor to raise a credit of about £250,000,000 to meet non-recurring extraordinary expenditure.—Reuter.

7.30 a.m. EDITION.

FIRE AND SWORD IN BELGIUM

GREAT GERMAN ADVANCE.

BATTLE NEAR LIEGE.

TOWNS ABLAZE.

POPULATION CUT UP.

GERMAN AIRMAN KILLED.

FROM OUR SPECIAL CORRESPONDENT.

MAASTRICHT (in Holland, near the Belgian frontier), Tuesday Evening.

(By telephone to Amsterdam.)

The Belgian frontier town of Visé, about eight miles from Maastricht, was taken by a body of German infantry and artillery this afternoon.

An engagement took place and lasted several hours.

The retreating Belgians blew up a bridge over the Meuse, but German sappers, covered by heavy artillery fire, built a new bridge and crossed the river.

Visé is practically destroyed.

Firing occurred throughout the day and was heard in all the surrounding towns.

LIEGE FIGHTING.

From Our Own Correspondent.

BRUSSELS, Tuesday, 6 p.m.

I am informed by the War Office that Liège and its forts are defending themselves energetically.

BRUSSELS, Wednesday.

A stubborn battle has been fought on the outskirts of Liège, where 80,000 Germans attempted to force their advance across Belgium and were engaged by the Liège militia, who after a fierce encounter so harassed the German troops on the right that they were forced to retire.—Exchange Telegraph Company.

LIEGE, Tuesday.

The Germans, hindered by the destroyed bridges, viaducts, and railways, have been compelled to make for the north and have violated Dutch territory at Tilburg.

They crossed the Meuse at Eysden. The 10th army corps is said to be at Eysden, the 7th, 40,000 strong, at Verviers, and the 6th at a place unknown.

Visé and Argenteau are in flames, the Germans having set fire to them. Civilians are reported to have fired on the Germans, who are reported to have decimated the population of Visé.

A hundred thousand Germans are marching on Liège, where an attack is expected to-morrow.

A wounded German officer who was captured expressed great astonishment at the resistance which the Germans were finding in Belgium. They had been assured, he said, in Berlin that no opposition would be encountered in Belgium.

A German airman has been killed.—Reuter.

GERMANS IN GREAT FORCE.

ATTACK ALL ALONG THE FRONTIER.

From Our Own Correspondent.

PARIS, Tuesday.

News has just reached the French Government that the Germans have invaded Belgium in great force.

Numbers of men in armoured motorcars and trains have entered the country near Visé, facing the great fortress of Liège, which dominates the Meuse valley, blowing up bridges.

The German attack is developing all along the Belgian frontier.

From Our Own Correspondent.

ROTTERDAM, Tuesday.

A correspondent of the Rotterdam *Courant* who stood on a hill at Vaals almost at the point where the frontiers of Holland, Belgium, and Germany meet, says he saw 30,000 Germans enter Belgium. The invaders issued proclamations declaring that they had come to assist Belgium, and several villagers welcomed them.

"WILL ENGLAND DELAY?"

KING ALBERT'S SUPREME APPEAL TO THE EMPIRE.

From Our Own Correspondent.

BRUSSELS, Tuesday.

King Albert was cheered to the echo to-day when he entered Parliament to address the united Chambers. His Majesty said:

"We are determined on the greatest sacrifices to defend our beloved country. David has faced Goliath. In the last twenty-four hours we have blown up and destroyed bridges, tunnels, and private property to the value of £40,000,000 to stop the advance of the cowardly aggressors who sought to make us buy peace at the price of our honour.

"We are doing the duty imposed upon us by international obligations. Will England delay to do hers until Belgium is turned into a gigantic cemetery in which will be buried our dead and her national honour; and while I, through this Chamber, make this supreme appeal to the great British nation and to the whole of the British Empire, Liège and her sister forts are keeping the flag of our national honour flying?

"Now and in view of every eventuality our valiant youth is ready. In the name of the nation I address to them a fraternal salutation. But one duty is theirs—an obstinate resistance.

"The moment is now for deeds."

An indescribable ovation greeted this declaration, which was made in firm and decisive tones. The Socialist leaders joined in the tempests of applause.

After the departure of the King and Queen, the Premier, Baron de Broqueville, made the following statement:—

"By accepting the German demands we would sacrifice the honour of the nation. Germany informed us at six o'clock this morning that she sees herself compelled to carry out military plans even with the use of force.

"We can be conquered, but not crushed and never reduced to submission."

GERMAN TAVERNS SACKED.

From Our Own Correspondent.

ANTWERP, Tuesday, 11.10 p.m.

Patriotic demonstrations are being held all over the town to-night. Manifestations have been made against the larger German-owned shops and hotels, which had to hoist the Belgian flag to appease the crowd. Several small German taverns near the harbour were sacked, and other German establishments are now being guarded by the military.

7.30 a.m. EDITION.

30 GERMANS DROWNED.

TORPEDO BOAT SUNK.

FROM OUR SPECIAL CORRESPONDENT.

COPENHAGEN, Tuesday, 11.25 p.m.

A German torpedo-boat to-day suddenly sank at the Gjedser Lighthouse, six miles from Gjedser, off the south Danish coast.

From the lighthouse it was observed that some sailors jumped overboard when the torpedo-boat sank, and a boat was despatched for assistance. It picked up a few sailors.

Thirty officers and men were drowned. The survivors declared that the boiler on board the torpedo-boat exploded.

BOMBS FROM THE AIR.

GERMAN AIRMAN OVER FRENCH FRONTIER TOWN.

From Our Own Correspondent.

PARIS, Monday Night.

A German aeroplane appeared to-day over Luneville, an important garrison town on the French frontier, and dropped three bombs, causing some damage but no loss of life.

Tuesday, 8.30 p.m.

The Germans have entered the village of Moineville, near Nancy. They have shot the village priest.

PARIS, Tuesday.

A German company is reported to be in French territory near Mars-la-Tour, the scene of one of the most sanguinary battles of the war of 1870.—Reuter.

Mars-la-Tour is a French village fourteen miles south-west of the German fortress of Metz.

GERMAN NAVAL RAID.

MEDITERRANEAN PORTS SHELLED.

From Our Own Correspondent.

PARIS, Tuesday, 3.50 p.m.

It is stated at the Ministry of Foreign Affairs that the German cruiser Breslau has bombarded Bona and Bougie, on the Algerian coast.

After firing sixty shells the warship sailed to the west.

Tuesday, 8.30 p.m.

The Breslau has also bombarded Philippeville, approaching under the Russian flag.

PARIS, Tuesday.

The Governor-General of Algeria reports that at four o'clock this morning a four-funnelled cruiser, thought to be the German cruiser Breslau, discharged eight broadsides at the town of Bona, sixty shells being fired. One man was killed and some houses were damaged.

She then steamed towards the west.—Reuter.

The Breslau is a small cruiser. She was last heard of in the Adriatic. She has twelve 4.1in. guns.

WARSHIP ON THE WATCH.

ST. PETERSBURG, Tuesday.

The following telegram has been received here from Tokio:—

"Yesterday a German warship was observed in the Strait of Tsushima watching the ships of the Russian Volunteer Fleet. The Japanese Fleet is quite ready to put to sea."—Reuter.

Tsushima was the scene of the last naval battle, nine years ago, when the Japanese destroyed the Russian Baltic Fleet.

BURNING VILLAGES.

GERMANS FALLING BACK BEFORE THE RUSSIANS.

ST. PETERSBURG, Tuesday.

The Russian troops have established contact with the enemy along the greater part of the Russo-German frontier. A reconnaissance has been made on the Bialla and Borzymmen front. The German troops have fallen back a day's march, burning the villages over an enormous stretch of country.—Reuter.

ALL-NIGHT SCENES.

DEMONSTRATING CROWDS ROUND THE PALACE

Shortly after eleven o'clock last night the King and Queen appeared on the balcony of Buckingham Palace, and the enthusiasm of the crowd was tremendous. At 1.30 this morning the Mall was packed with people marching and singing, and there was still a large number at 3 a.m.

All through the evening there had been crowds waiting in the streets for definite tidings of the approaching conflict. Bands of men and women went marching up and down, singing and waving flags. Motors decorated with the French and English flags paraded through the streets, with rolling cheers following them.

Soon after midnight the news of the declaration of war spread, and in Piccadilly-circus there was a scene of the greatest enthusiasm. The tension of the past few days had become intolerable and, terrible though the news might be, it came as a positive relief. The National Anthem and the Marseillaise were sung.

A great roaring cheer of defiance was the answer of a vast crowd in Trafalgar-square to the news. One vast patriotic shout rent the air. Union Jacks were waved, often in company with the tricolour of France, and processions of people marched round the foot of the Nelson column cheering wildly and singing national airs. Hooting motor-cars picked their way through the mass, with people piled on the roof and all the passengers waving Union Jacks. The scene was one of extraordinary and surpassing enthusiasm.

EMPRESS AS NURSE.

From Our Own Correspondent.

COPENHAGEN, Tuesday.

The Russian Ambassador at Berlin, M. Sverbeieff, arrived here to-day with the Grand Duchess Xenia's son-in-law, Prince Ile Youssoupoff, who had been arrested in Berlin and afterwards released.

Princess Youssoupoff was seriously shocked by the Prince's unexpected arrest, and had to be carried [...] from the train [...]

THE NATION CALLS FOR LORD KITCHENER.

IS LORD HALDANE DELAYING WAR PREPARATIONS?

WHAT IS HE DOING AT THE WAR OFFICE?

What is the Lord Chancellor doing at the War Office? Lord Haldane is, as everybody knows, an excellent and admirable Lord Chancellor, a great lawyer, and an extremely fluent and voluble orator, but why is he occupying himself at this moment with affairs that have nothing to do with the Woolsack?

We had news on Monday that Lord Kitchener, without doubt the greatest available military organiser, had been suddenly recalled to London when on board a Channel steamer; and it was generally believed and hoped that it was the intention of the Government to ask him to take charge of the War Office in this great crisis. Public opinion, which is strongly in favour of the adoption of this course, was pleased and satisfied, and it was everywhere supposed that at last we should see the right man in the right place.

But the fact is that for the last two days it is not Lord Kitchener, nor even Mr. Asquith, the Secretary of State for War, who has been the presiding genius at the War Office, but Lord Haldane! Mr. Asquith is, of course, very fully occupied with matters of the gravest importance, and it was explained to the few people who knew of Lord Haldane's presence at the War Office that the Lord Chancellor is "assisting Mr. Asquith." The fact is that he has been gently but very firmly assuming control of the military preparations. It is feared that he is delaying them.

It is very freely rumoured that at Sunday morning's Cabinet meeting Lord Haldane was bitterly opposed to any war preparations at all. His well-known friendship with the Kaiser and his admiration for all things German—a sympathy begotten of his German education—led him, no doubt, to believe that German aggression was impossible, and it was not till the afternoon of that day, when news had been received of the German attack on Luxemburg, that he became very reluctantly convinced that Germany meant business.

OFFICIAL DENIALS.

Naturally the Lord Chancellor's activity at the War Office led to the belief that it was intended to make him Secretary of State for War when Mr. Asquith relinquishes that office, which he only assumed temporarily when Colonel Seely resigned. It is generally understood that the Prime Minister, burdened as he is with the chief responsibility for British policy and the general supervision of all departments, will not continue to hold the office much longer.

To allay public anxiety, which was much increased last night by the news of Lord Haldane's presence at the War Office, two official denials were issued during the evening.

The Press Association was "officially informed that there is no truth in the report that Lord Haldane is going to the War Office either as Secretary of State or to assist Mr. Asquith."

The Central News was also officially informed that it was not true that Lord Haldane would take over temporarily Mr. Asquith's duties.

If these official denials are truly inspired we can only ask again, "What is the Lord Chancellor doing at the War Office?"

LORD MORLEY'S RESIGNATION.

Lord Morley's resignation is definitely announced. Mr. Burns's offer of resignation is still under consideration.

SCENE IN THE CHAMBER.

FRENCH CHEERS FOR BRITAIN.

From Our Own Correspondent.

PARIS, Tuesday.

Pale-faced and stern, tightly buttoned up in his frock-coat, M. Viviani, the French Premier, this afternoon read to a silent Chamber of Deputies the declaration of the Government's policy and paid a striking tribute to the loyalty shown in the crisis by England.

Roars of applause interrupted his speech at the first reference to the "faithful ally" and Sir Edward Grey. To a person familiar with French politics the sight of this Chamber, usually so divided and now cheering like one man, was a revelation. It brought conclusive proof that before the German attack all parties in France have become united.

Quotations from Sir E. Grey's speech were greeted with tumultuous applause, and the ovation to Great Britain at the conclusion of the Premier's statement was one of those things one can never forget.

When the Chamber assembled the silence under the great dome of the Palais Bourbon was that of a church, for the session began with the reading of the funeral orations in honour of M. Jaurès, the murdered Socialist leader, by M. Paul Deschanel, President of the Chamber. "There are no enemies here now," he concluded. "There are only Frenchmen mourning one of their finest [...] men."

PARIS, [...]

Enthusiastic tributes [...] England by the [...]

Figaro [...] "Hurrah for [...] Grey's speech! Five [...] with the barbarians [...] gods drive mad [...] destroy."

WHERE THE FLEETS WILL MEET.

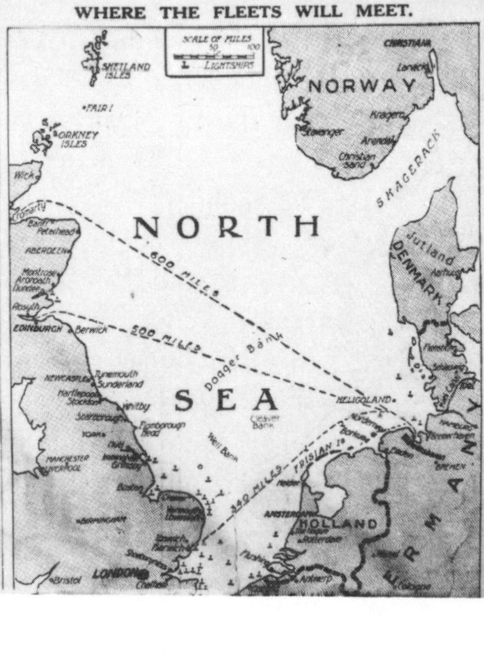

Recruits on pay parade Trafalgar Square, August 1914

cheering and laughter; the sky was alight with bursting fireworks. And Sir
Edward Grey, gloomily contemplating them, said, "The lights are going out all
over Europe: we shall not see them lit again in our lifetime."

Those who, like Mrs. Bridges, were buying up stocks of food in anticipation
of shortages created havoc in the shops. They came with cars, with barrels and
dustbins to carry off as much food as could be crammed in. Only an official plea
to "act as you always act" restored some sort of normality. Afraid of a similar
rush for money, the banks remained closed until the end of Bank Holiday week.
Soon after they reopened, they dealt out a new kind of money—paper notes for
one pound and ten shillings. Gone forever was the golden sovereign, replaced by
the flimsy, grubby "Bradburys," as they were called from the name printed on

them of the Joint Permanent Secretary to the Treasury. Another drastic innovation was the Defence of the Realm Act, immediately known as DORA and caricatured as a ferocious-looking maiden aunt in Victorian costume. DORA clamped down on the civilian population, imposing the threat of court-martial on anyone caught communicating with the enemy, spying, or causing "alarm or disaffection." In the next year "she" would earn great unpopularity by decreeing drastically shortened drinking hours for public houses, which had previously stayed happily open almost as long as their patrons wanted to drink. Unpopular the move may have been, but its effects were good, reducing the heavy drinking and its ugly consequences that had been a feature of Britain since time immemorial. The King set an example by banishing alcohol from the royal table; but the Bellamys did not follow his lead.

Belgium was the chief topic of conversation in the early weeks of the war. The phrase "gallant little Belgium" began with a *Punch* cartoon showing a small Belgian peasant boy defending a gate marked "No Thoroughfare" from the threat of a ponderous booted German armed with a club. The German was to

German mobilization—no lack of enthusiasm

An apprehensive Prince of Wales

The Huguot family billeted at the Bellamys

make countless reappearances in cartoons, posters, every kind of propaganda. He was always fat, spectacled, thickly moustachioed, coarse, and brutal. Kaiser Wilhelm, Queen Victoria's beloved grandson, came out in what were now accepted as his true colours, a tomcat aggressor in a spiked helmet and the costume of Lohengrin, breathing fire and brimstone, sometimes captioned as "the Mad Dog of Europe" or "The Beast of the Apocalypse."

It seemed from news reports that the German "rape of Belgium" was a very real thing. The neutral country was ravaged, her people ruthlessly killed. In the city of Namur alone 1,949 civilians died and 3,000 houses were destroyed. The same pattern was followed in every town the invaders entered, hostages being shot wholesale whenever resistance was shown. Lady Prudence staged a slightly ludicrous pageant, in which Ruby represented Belgium and she herself the

"Spymania . . . swept the country like influenza."

jackbooted Hun, only one of the many to be organized in the drawing rooms of Britain. Refugees poured into towns on the east coast and were rapturously received by sympathizers. But the case of the Huguot family's billeting upon the Bellamys was fairly typical. Hosts' sympathy tended to melt under the pressure of life with evacuees whose ways were foreign to them, and the Belgians eventually drifted into settlements where they could speak their own language and live the sort of life they knew.

The sad story of the Schoenfelds was a common one, too. Mr. Hudson's hostility to the German-born baker and his family was only too typical of those infected with the "spymania" that swept the country like influenza. Everybody with an even faintly German name was suspected by the gullible as a spy. Britons, who in normal circumstances would behave rationally, banded together like wolves to attack the houses, shops, property, and persons of the unhappy "spies." The campaign against them went on, fed by the press and in particular the unscrupulous editor of *John Bull*, Horatio Bottomley. The Prime Minister, Herbert Henry Asquith, would eventually give in to popular demand and ordain that enemy aliens between the ages of seventeen and forty-five should be interned in special camps where, presumably, they would be able to do no harm. Almost incredibly, one of those to suffer from the "Hun spy" label was the First Sea Lord of the Admiralty, Prince Louis Alexander of Battenburg, whose brother had married Queen Victoria's daughter Princess Beatrice. Press agitation forced him to resign. In 1917 he relinquished his German titles and changed his name to Mountbatten. In the course of time a naval officer called Mountbatten, great-nephew to Prince Louis, would marry the princess who was to become Queen Elizabeth II.

But in 1914 the only good Germans were, in the popular phrase, dead ones. Of course, they would soon be licked, thought the optimists, by our brave Tommies, and the war would certainly be over by Christmas.

Prince Louis Alexander of Battenburg, First Sea Lord of the Admiralty, bids farewell to the British Navy.

The creators of "Tipperary": Harry Williams, Bert Feldman, and Jack Judge

CHAPTER NINE

Total War: 1914 – 1918

The optimists were mistaken. By Christmas shells fired from German cruisers in the North Sea had killed 137 civilians and injured 592 more in the northeast coast towns of Whitby, Scarborough, and Hartlepool, and the first German bomb fell on Dover on Christmas Eve. Nobody had thought such a thing could happen. It seemed the more impossible because the towns attacked were holiday resorts, where so many children had played that fine summer. Beaches and buildings were scarred with shot, boardinghouses and hotels damaged and windowless. It was one of the dismal surprises of the months following the declaration of war.

There had been so much enthusiasm at first. The British Expeditionary Force of regular army troops had left England for France amid cheers and the singing of patriotic songs. Words like *duty* and *honour* were much in use. Popular heroes were created—Sir John French, Commander of the British Expeditionary Force; Lord Kitchener, whose bristling moustaches, piercing eyes, and dramatically pointing finger appeared on the most famous of the recruiting posters. Lord Kitchener was under no illusions about the seriousness of the situation. The war, he said, would last four years, a prophecy that proved to be correct. He banned war correspondents from the front, but one correspondent managed to get a dire piece of news released on August 30: The battle of Liège, the first of the war, had been lost, and the British and French armies were in retreat.

England Expects
every man to do his
DUTY

and We'll all do it.

1914 recruiting poster

A wartime revue in London

But to the crowds of civilian men queuing to enlist, the mud, blood, and misery in France were quite unknown and unimaginable. Men of all classes, boys pretending to be older than they were were keen to start drilling, to get into khaki. They were impatient at the shortage of uniforms and equipment; they enjoyed changing city wear and boiler suits and their old ordinary lives for entirely new ones. Their excitement was summed up in one line of a poem by Rupert Brooke: "Now, God be thanked Who has matched us with this hour. . . ."

On a lower cultural level than that of the poet but one much more typical of the English at war, the theatre and music halls were doing their bit in characteristic style. There were new wartime revues in London—*England Expects, Business as Usual, On Duty.* Songs, sentimental and rousing: "Kiss me Goodbye," "Soldier Boy," "Are We Downhearted? No!" "Sister Susie's Sewing Shirts for Soldiers," and, most popular of all, a ditty the irrepressible Miss

Florrie Forde had introduced early in 1914. It was about an Irish boy in London who found himself "a long way from Tipperary." A music-hall comedian who was a fishmonger in his spare time had written it some years before and had had it rejected by several publishers until it was finally, and unenthusiastically, bought by Bert Feldman for five shillings.

By the end of 1914 it was selling sheet copies at the rate of ten thousand a day, increasingly in demand, for in August the British Expeditionary Force (BEF) had been singing it as they landed in France.

> *It's a long way to Tipperary,*
> *It's a long way to go . . .*

A simple, rather silly song had achieved an immortality unequalled even by the hymn of Henry V's soldiers after Agincourt.

Silliness of a peculiarly English kind—wryly facetious—was present in the unofficial marching songs that crept into the vocabulary of the troops. More emotional nations might declaim, pray, weep, or flag-wave, but Britain went to war to the sedate tune of "The Church's One Foundation" with singularly unecclesiastical words. The Fred Karno of the song managed a variety group.

> *We are Fred Karno's Army, the ragtime infantry,*
> *We cannot fight, we cannot march, what bloody good are we?*
> *And when we get to Berlin, the Kaiser he will say,*
> *'Hoch hoch, mein Gott, what a bloody rotten lot*
> *Are the ragtime infantry!'*

Another song requested the military authorities to

> *Call out my mother, my sister and my brother,*
> *But for God's sake don't send me!*

To such songs men like Edward Barnes, the Bellamys' footman, cheerfully drilled, and in France James Bellamy, from the military HQ, heard them singing in the trenches.

The tide of victory turned away from Germany at the Battle of the Marne, early in September, and gave the Allies new hope. A few days later the Battle of the Aisne, a protracted and bloody struggle, featured a new German weapon, the Krupp high-angle howitzer, whose shells tore deeply into the earth and whose breath was thick, choking, poisonous smoke.

Darkness reigned in London. All windows had to be covered by blinds so that not the slightest chink of light showed (Mr. Hudson was particularly careful about this). The glass of street lamps was painted over for the rare times when they were lit. Only the shining, twisting Thames would show Zeppelins, when they came over, where London lay.

The first terrible battle of Ypres brought mourning to Britain. The BEF lost over 54,000 officers and men. At home millions of civilians were training to replace them, and men from the colonies were arriving, Rose's Australian ex-fiancé Gregory included. It was not enough, said many. Voluntary recruitment sent the valiant to the front and allowed the shirkers to stay at home, as comfortably as their consciences would let them. As winter rains in Flanders were swamping the trenches and shell holes, reducing the Allies' terrain to a horrible swamp, the authorities in Britain were seriously thinking of introducing conscription.

James is called to arms.

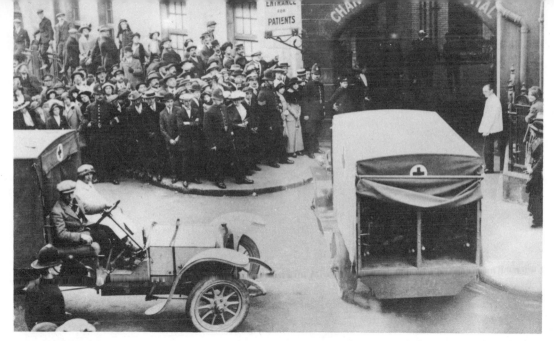

Wounded from the Western Front arriving at Charing Cross Hospital in motor ambulances, September 1914

No bells were rung in church steeples on New Year's Eve, 1914.

It was ironic that in the early months of 1915 readers of the *Strand* were absorbed in Sir Arthur Conan Doyle's new Sherlock Holmes story, for its title was *The Valley of Fear*. England was learning to know a fear she had never known before—fear of attack from the skies. Zeppelins, those clumsy, lumbering airships whose prewar existence had alarmed such natural pessimists as Mr. Hudson, proved to be as great a menace as had been feared. To do the Kaiser justice, he had not been anxious to let London be bombed, and when he finally agreed he stipulated that his airmen must attack military targets only, leaving alone historic buildings and royal palaces. How could the grandson of Queen Victoria have permitted their destruction? Besides, when he marched into London in the foreseeable future it would be to take up his quarters in Buckingham Palace.

They began with East Anglia. The first bombs fell on Great Yarmouth, on the harbour where Nelson had landed in 1800, and on King's Lynn, Norfolk, an ancient town with a famous corn and cattle market and as much of a Franciscan friary as Henry VIII had allowed to remain. Other towns in the area suffered later. Those who had first rushed out to look for the monstrous attackers soon learned to take shelter instead. There was nothing much to be seen, except the airship's lights, but its engines sounded like the growling and roaring of immense tigers, and the crash of the bombs was a louder and more terrible noise

Searchlights on Old Lambeth Bridge

than England had ever heard before. An observer described one of the Zeppelins as the biggest sausage he had ever seen in his life, and, irresistibly, there were jokes about German sausages and dachshunds and revivals of a popular Victorian song:

> *Oh vere, oh vere ist mein leetle dog gone?*
> *Oh vere, oh vere can he be?*
> *Mit his tail cut short und his ears cut long,*
> *Oh vere, oh vere is he?*

Londoners were still curious rather than frightened when the Zeppelins came to the capital in September. They ran out to see the airships that were dropping bombs on the city, destroying riverside warehouses and killing thirty-eight people. Tower Bridge, a natural target with its twin turrets and graceful spans, escaped, but Liverpool Street Station caught the last bombs of the first raid. In the next attack, the audience at one of the Melville Brothers' melo-dramas in the Lyceum Theatre were literally shaken by the crash of bombs in Wellington Street outside and the screams of the injured. Twenty people died. And Britain had found no reply to the Zeppelin.

Another terrible weapon threatened at sea. In January 1915, the month of the first Zeppelin raids, the battleship *Formidable* was torpedoed by the German submarine U.24. In February Germany declared British home waters to be a war zone and announced that in future she would be using submarines to sink merchant ships. By the end of the year she had sunk 259. Unprepared but resourceful,

The funeral of the Lusitania *victims: the scene at the graveyard*

Warning of an impending air raid

The sinking of the Lusitania. *The picture includes a facsimile of the medal struck by Germany to commemorate the event.*

Britain mustered small craft of all kinds (she would do the same at Dunkirk in another war) to reinforce the coastal patrols. The little ships did their best, but Germany had a shock in store for the world that no gallantry could have prevented. Mr. Hudson read to a horrified servants' hall the news of the sinking by torpedo of the Cunard liner *Lusitania*. The German Embassy in Washington had, almost incredibly, announced that Germany intended to sink the great ship, but so unlikely did this seem that few passengers cancelled their sailings. On May 7, off the Old Head of Kinsale, County Cork, the liner went down, her side shattered, and with her went over 1,000 men, women, and children.

There were famous names on the death roll—A. G. Vanderbilt, Charles Frohman, the theatrical manager, and Charles Klein, the playwright—but it was the child victims whom Britain lamented most. The magazine *Sphere* offered a poignant drawing of the ship's deck just before the sinking: a passenger points to a disturbance in the water, a children's nurse distractedly follows his gaze, and her little charges innocently play by their mother's side. "Murder on the High Seas!" shrieked the caption. The *Lusitania* was only one of several liners to be sunk by German "frightfulness," as it was beginning to be called, and the tragedy started a train of resentment against everything German, which led to the internment of aliens, including the unfortunate Schoenfelds.

The year 1915 was one of mounting horrors. In the Second Battle of Ypres, fought from April 22 to May 13, British forces captured the strategically important Hill 60. The Germans, in trying to recapture it, let loose "great volumes of asphyxiating gas, which caused nearly all our men along a front of about 400 yards to be immediately struck down by its fumes. The splendid courage with which the leaders rallied their men, and subdued the natural tendency to panic . . . combined with the prompt intervention of supports, once more drove the enemy back." The wind had favoured the Allied forces during the first gas attack, but the weather moved over to the enemy side with a changed wind, and on May 5 Hill 60 was back in German hands.

Belated protection against poison gas

The British invention of the tank could have shortened the war but for the resistance of diehard cavalry generals.

Britain retaliated with gas at the Battle of Loos in September. France followed with phosgene. Both sides used yperite, which could poison a whole area for days, corrode skin, and contaminate clothing. A badly gassed man would never be the same again. At best he would speak with a grotesquely hoarse, squeaky voice coming from damaged lungs, to the end of a life that was all too often shortened drastically. Gas was a filthy weapon, widely condemned as a breach of the laws of war, and it was not even an effective one, serving only to baffle briefly. It was superseded on the Allies' side by a British invention, the tank, which might have been an immense advantage had diehard generals brought up in the cavalry tradition not been too slow to make use of its possibilities.

Lord Kitchener, now War Minister, raised a volunteer army of two million men, men who as yet knew nothing of what they would have to face. Young playboys like Georgina's friends still thought of war as "glorious," in spite of the sights to be seen when a hospital train arrived at one of London's stations: soldiers maimed, blinded, unrecognizable in heavy bandages, sometimes literally dying. It was no wonder that the Georginas of London, pretty girls who had only thought of themselves as consolers of officers on leave, became suddenly inspired to join the Red Cross and go through the arduous, far from romantic training that would, if they could stay the course, take them out to France to nurse in base hospitals. They would see sights more horrible than they could have imagined in any nightmare, do things they had no notion they could do, work harder than they had ever worked before or ever would again. There were those who cracked under the strain, but by far the greater number went on nursing. Grisly though the experience was, it would benefit them in the end; and war was to revolutionize the position of women in general.

Kitchener was taking away the men, so many of whom would never come back. They must be replaced somehow, either by men over serving age or by

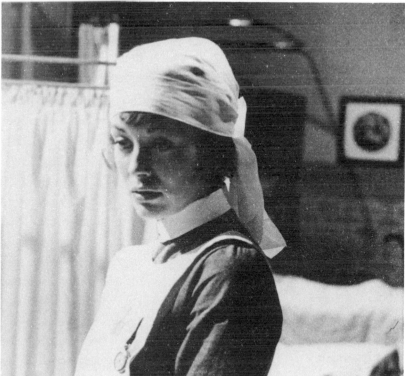

"The Georginas of London . . . became suddenly inspired to join the Red Cross."

Women munitions workers in Woolwich Arsenal

women. (Those men who were too old to fight and were doing a necessary civilian job in factory or office wore a badge inscribed "On War Service." It spared them embarrassing gifts of white feathers from patriotic women on the lookout for "shirkers.") The cue for the women came after the fall of the Asquith Liberal government in May 1915 and the appointment, under Asquith now as coalition leader, of the brilliant David Lloyd George to the job of Minister of Munitions. A master of organization, he amassed an enormous Ministry, swept away Kitchener's limited distribution of army contracts and handed them out to small firms as well as the established large ones. New factories were opened. Others, such as those producing textiles, were turned over to munitions, while under Lloyd George's firm control strikes were as far as possible banned and the resentful trades unions curbed; they had objected strongly to the employment of women and unskilled men. The result was startling. Not only were the Army and Navy supplied with the armaments they so desperately needed, but the demand for workers virtually banished unemployment and rescued poorly paid workers from their menial jobs. A girl like Ruby, working for small wages and with no prospect of promotion, would not hesitate to go into munitions where she could earn three or four times as much money, though the job was dangerous. Those who handled gunpowder for shells had to wear special gloves and masks, and even so their faces would be likely to turn yellow from the fumes. At the worst, they could be blown up as Ruby's mates were in the 1917 Silvertown explosion, which killed 69 women and injured 450. Many women were so unused to machinery that they would cry when taken off a process they had painstakingly learnt and transferred to an unfamiliar one.

Women began to change in appearance. Skirts had to be shorter—long ones were quite impracticable in industry—though they still stayed below the knee. Girls in the Woman's Land Army strode about in boots and trousers. The "shell girls" cut their hair short, for long hair might have caught in machinery and scalped them. By 1917, when war seemed almost a normal state of things, women were in uniform for the first time in history. The WAACs (Women's Auxiliary Army Corps) wore neat costumes, hip-length belted tunics, and

Policewomen of the First World War

An aeroplane worker in a Midlands munitions factory

Women undertook all kinds of unfamiliar work as part of the war effort.

A woman tram driver in Lowestoft

London bus conductorettes

calf-length skirts, their wide hats turned up at the side like those of the Australian troops, and their sisters the WRNS (Women's Royal Naval Service) and WRAFs (Women's Royal Air Force) were similarly garbed. In contrast, they were ultrafeminine in the evenings, on the arms of servicemen on leave, in their tantalizingly short frocks revealing silk stockings and high-heeled shoes. They smoked in public instead of in private, as they had once done. They liked to be called daring, and magazine-story writers described their heroines as delicious, adorable, wild-rose-like. They drank cocktails, the ultimate in "fast" drinks; they swore, to the extent of using very mild expletives. One comedienne, who had used the word "damn" to give point to a stage story, overheard a lady in the front stalls observe to her friend, "Disgusting!" "Yes, dear," replied the friend, "but I believe she's an American."

They went to theatres when their boy friends or husbands came back to "Blighty" for a blessed respite from the trenches to see George Robey and Vi Loraine in *The Bing Boys Are Here* or *The Better 'Ole,* a "fragment from France" with music. Hazel Bellamy and her airman friend Jack Dyson went to a night club, one of the many that were springing up in the West End of London, where bands played the tunes of the time: "You Called Me Baby Doll a Year Ago," "If You Were the Only Girl in the World," or something from the popular musical comedy *The Arcadians*. When they danced, it was to steps introduced by the Americans Vernon and Irene Castle, sponsors of the tango, perhaps the Castle Walk, the Lula-Fado, Tato Polka, Braziliane, or Hesitation. They danced closely and intimately, like people who had only a short time together before what might be a final parting. In a darkened, sandbagged, camouflaged London one snatched at any fragment of gaiety. And if morals declined, as has been said, it was only what has always happened under the stress of war, and in this case it was also a natural reaction to the sudden freedom from the restrictions of Victorian and Edwardian times.

Life in Britain was increasingly austere throughout 1916 and 1917. Families were losing their servants, as women like Rose went off to be bus conductor-ettes, and men too old to serve emulated Mr. Hudson and became Special Constables. Women who had never done a day's work in their lives found themselves shopping and cleaning, and everybody queued for the goods in short supply, which were many. Blockades at sea by German U-boats meant that starvation might not be far away. Lloyd George's Ministry of Food imposed a voluntary ration scheme that worked only imperfectly. Bread, potatoes, and sugar were particularly scarce, butter and margarine were almost unobtainable, and special classes in wartime meatless cookery produced some unpalatable results. (Mrs. Bridges tried the experiment on her household but only once.) Allotments appeared, green fertile vegetable plots where wasted land had been before, for the cultivation of food that could not be bought, and a Daylight Saving Bill gave an extra hour of light for working. Everybody was singing, whistling, and humming the song "Keep the Home Fires Burning," written by a very young and handsome composer serving with the Royal Naval Volunteer Reserve, Ivor Novello Davies, but in fact it was easier said than done, for there was a serious shortage of coal, and in 1917 it was rationed.

With national austerity went national mourning. There were few families in Britain who had not lost someone—husband, brother, father, sweetheart—in the bitter struggle being waged from Calais to the farthest tip of the Turkish Empire on land and sea. Millions of men, "the flower of young English manhood," it was said, were butchered in four years of useless fighting, shattered by machine-gun fire, dying on the barbed-wire entanglements of no-man's-land. A report from the battlefield of the Somme, possibly the bloodiest battle ever fought, told Britain that after an Allied victory "one party came by at a quick march, away up to take their share in our triumph, and a jingling song was on their lips":

> *We beat 'em on the Marne,*
> *We beat 'em on the Aisne,*
> *We gave them hell at Neuve Chapelle,*
> *And here we are again.*

The battlefield at Ypres

No-man's-land, the Western Front

But this was morale-sustaining propaganda. Far more typical was a grim song of the trenches:

> *If you want to find the Major, we know where 'e is,*
> *'E's 'anging on the old barbed wire.*

The horrors that sickened the once-military-minded James Bellamy into saying, "There can't be any argument, any dispute, that's worth so many people's lives and so much blood" were softened in news reports and in the letters written by company commanders to the nearest relatives of the dead. They were said to have died instantly with no pain. Rudyard Kipling was among those who received a War Office telegram saying that his only son was missing. For him the dreadful suspense of not knowing John's fate lasted two years; then he heard confirmation that John was dead and buried at Loos in a shell hole. He expressed something of his own suffering, and the suffering of his countrymen, in a poem written soon after the news came. It had the despairing refrain "But who shall return us our children?"

Those who came back from the Western Front and other battlefields were all too often maimed, blind, gassed, or shell-shocked. Able-bodied men who refused to fight on moral or religious grounds were harshly condemned as "Conchies" (conscientious objectors), jeered at, and put through an inquisition about their motives. If they agreed to undertake some kind of non-militant war work they escaped the fate of those who did not; *they* were put under military law, jailed, and brutally treated. By the middle of 1917 Britain was a country of old people, women, children, and invalids, and even they were menaced by the new German weapon, the Gotha bomber, a great four-engine machine far more deadly than the clumsy Zeppelins. Several "Zepps" had been shot down near London in 1916, amid rejoicings. Photographs of the machines' burned-out skeletons delighted newspaper readers. "The mass looked like the glassless roof of Olympia after being dented by a huge hammer." To make things even worse a great influenza epidemic had spread over Europe, some said from the filthy trenches of France, to kill thousands of Britons—the worst infection since the Great Plague. Hazel Bellamy was one of its victims, and James was left a widower.

On June 13, 1917, a fleet of Gotha bombing planes bombed London, killing many civilians, including children at an East End school. In July they came back, bringing more death and destruction with them. For eight more months the raids continued, foreshadowing Hitler's attacks in 1940; and then, as in the later war, people took to sheltering on platforms in the Underground stations until the shrill bugles of Boy Scout messengers sounded the All Clear.

Kitchener was dead, drowned at sea in 1916. Haig, Jellicoe, Beatty, France's General Joffre, General Allenby in Palestine, T. E. Lawrence in Arabia, the brilliant brain of Winston Churchill, new Minister of Munitions, all seemed powerless against the might of the German war machine. A German propaganda poster showed a spectral spiked-helmeted figure looming over the Dover cliffs. Worse and worse news came home: Russia had collapsed and disintegrated in revolution, Italy had been crushed by German-Austrian forces at Caporetto, the French Army was exhausted, Roumania overrun. The omens were poor for Allied survival.

But Germany, too, was tired and hungry. General Ludendorff, the strategist of the time, chanced everything in a great attempt to split the British 4th and

"The Yanks are coming!" 5th U.S. Marines in France, June 1917

5th armies from the French in March 1918. General Haig called on his men to fight "with their backs to the wall," and nobly they obeyed. The guns of France could be heard by now in London, not only in the Channel ports. One powerful card remained up the Allies' sleeve. In April 1917 the United States of America had entered the war. It had happened because, historians say, "the United States could no longer live in peace with such a nation as Germany had become." President Woodrow Wilson wanted to make the world "safe for democracy." The sinking of the *Lusitania* and other innocent passenger vessels had aroused national indignation. The die was cast; what remained to be decided was the organization. A great force of American troops must be raised, trained, despatched. The first batch, the American Expeditionary Force, left for Europe on May 28, 1917, and General Pershing planned to send at least 3,000,000 men, as well as vast supplies. American troops fought in thirteen major operations, gradually making clear to Germany that those in the American camp who had hoped for neutrality or enmity to the Allied cause were to be disappointed. To the strains of "Over There!" American soldiers joined the Allies in the last push that ended, amid incredulous relief, at "the eleventh hour of the eleventh day"—11:00 A.M. on November 11, 1918.

The legacy of Ypres

The troops celebrate the Armistice.

CHAPTER TEN

A Fit Country For Heroes to Live In

The lights had gone up again, but the blaze of glory people had expected when peace was announced was singularly lacking. When the first cheering was over there was present a curious anticlimactic feeling. They had lived war, talked war for four years. What was there to talk about now? Fiction about captured Germans and shot-down bombers continued to fill the magazines. Patriotic songs drew the most applause at concerts in aid of Lord Roberts' Fund—songs about the gallant boys of the Dover Patrol that had manned the "grey destroyers, the hornets of our Fleet" against German boats, Elgar's "Land of Hope and Glory" majestically delivered by the contralto Dame Clara Butt. It kept the spirits up to be able to pretend that the cheering was still going on.

The situation of the household at No. 165 was typical of many British families. Rose had lost her fiancé, killed at the Battle of the Somme. Hazel's lover, the air ace Jack Dyson, had been shot down. James had been seriously wounded in body and mind, and Edward would never be quite the same man again after suffering from shell shock. Richard had met and been attracted to the Scottish widow Virginia Hamilton in 1917. The death of her sailor son at Ostend had brought her and Richard closer together. Not long afterward they were married. Georgina, a frivolous little socialite when the war began, had

179

Hazel, a victim of the influenza epidemic

turned herself into a dedicated nurse, seeing sights and doing things that once would have been unthinkable to a girl of her protected background.

Ruby's return to her place as kitchen maid was less typical. Girls who had left domestic service for a well-paid factory job were usually unwilling to return to their former employment, having gained their independence and, if they were over thirty, the vote. Ironically, after all the campaigns and martyrdoms of the suffrage movement, it was the work of women in industry that finally won over the government to grant them, by means of the Sex Disqualification of Women Act of 1918, what they had fought for so long. At last woman was emancipated. "The vote to her," said a writer of the time, "is what the removal of the bandages from the feet is to the Chinese woman."

Edward and Daisy, now married, were determined to strike out for themselves as soon as Edward was discharged. Like so many others, they were soon disillusioned. Lloyd George had declared that postwar Britain should be "a fit country for heroes to live in," but the heroes were not finding themselves very warmly welcomed. Women had taken the jobs of many of them and were not to be dislodged. As munitions work ceased, unemployment began to rise, and not only ex-privates but their ex-officers found themselves lining up for menial jobs or trying to sell brushes at street doors. Their shabbily clad figures and shiny suitcases became a familiar sight, moving wearily from house to house, more often than not rejected, doors slammed in their faces. It was not what they had expected. A great wave of disillusion settled over the men who had longed to get home to "Blighty" and a return to normal living. "I am sorely troubled by the present widespread unemployment," declared King George in 1921, "which is causing so much suffering to so many of my people. It is my sincere hope that the efforts of my Ministers to alleviate the present and prevent future unemployment may be successful."

There was nowhere to set up house in comfort. A great housing shortage had set in, for building had come to a halt during the war. In Parliament, a proposal for "Council housing" was put forward, which was a development of the leafy, semirural Garden Suburb scheme on less aesthetic lines. The new Council

Former soldiers parade in Whitehall.

One of the new Council houses

houses were to be small, with low rents subsidized in part by government grant and in part by the authorities concerned. The scheme was put into action; a rash of Council estates began to spread all over the country. They were ugly little modern houses, adding themselves incongruously to villages and country towns, providing, however, cheap accommodation for the Edwards and Daisies who would have had none otherwise. And for the unemployed, Lloyd George proposed an Unemployed Workers' Dependents Fund, to be provided by a levy of twopence weekly on the employer, twopence on every male employee, and threepence paid by the state.

In the new little houses there would be a gas oven in the kitchen. Electric ovens were still regarded with suspicion. Dishwashers, washing machines, and electric irons were similarly shunned, even if the housewife could have afforded them. But any gadget likely to make housework easier, without blowing up in her face, was sought after, especially by those housewives whose servants had left them for outside work. In 1919 the humorous artist W. Heath Robinson drew a fancicul picture showing two intrepid gentlemen walking a clothesline to rescue a servant whose ladder had slipped while she was hanging out her washing. Heath Robinson's fanciful devices became a feature of English life.

While the poor and the less well off struggled along, young society people in Georgina's set reacted predictably to the aftermath of war. The young men who

"Iron nerve of senior members of the Alpine Club in preserving one of the few surviving domestic helps"

The smoking suit: "The women of the early Twenties . . . seemed determined to abolish the salient points of the female figure."

had been officers and the young women who had been nurses wanted to forget the horrors in a whirl of gaiety. "People are dancing as they have never danced before," reported the *Daily Mail* in 1919. The older generation was shocked to note that they were dancing without gloves, a thing at one time too vulgar to contemplate, and that girls were smoking openly and heavily instead of, as at one time, taking a furtive puff in their bedrooms. They roared about in noisy cars; they held fancy-dress parties from dusk till dawn. They were the beginnings of the Bright Young Things, the people whom a still very young man named Noel Coward would celebrate in immortal words and music.

The reaction of women to the end of the war was interestingly different from their reaction in 1947, when the ultrafeminine "New Look" was the complete negation of the mannish, uniform-type dress of the war years. The women of the early Twenties, or their fashion arbiters, seemed determined to abolish the salient points of the female figure. All-in-one foundation garments flattened out the bosom; the body appeared to be the same width all the way down, with a completely flat front ("boyish" was the contemporary, admiring description); draped sashes gave the appearance that the waist was somewhere just above the knees. The hemline had settled at an unbecoming spot above the ankle. It was perhaps the ugliest period of female dress that had ever existed, topped as it was by heads of preposterous waved hair. (The Nestlé wave had dominated hairdressing until 1914, when its German inventor, Karl Nessler, was interned; he escaped to America and made a fortune.) As for men, they looked more or less the same as they had always done. They always wore hats in the street—Trilby, bowler, top hat, or straw boater—and their shirts still had awkward detachable collars that fastened to the neck of the shirt with a stud.

From 1920 onwards they, the men in the street, would be moving in droves towards some sports arena, depending on the time of year, welcoming sport back after the wartime shutdown. In a contemporary cartoon the footballer was shown as next to Charlie Chaplin in popularity. All kinds of football matches,

The Hairdressing Fair of Fashion: three new styles

Suzanne Lenglen at Wimbledon

from those of the Football Association Amateur Cup to the great battles between such famous teams as the " 'Spurs," Wolverhampton Wanderers, Birmingham and Crystal Palace, were enthusiastically attended by well-behaved spectators, who sang quite seriously that lugubrious hymn "Abide with Me" at the beginning of a match.

In golf, 1921 saw America finally secure the English Open Golf Championship at St. Andrew's after many attempts. Jock Hutchison, of Scottish birth but American adoption, beat the English R. H. Wethered in a replay after a tie. At Wimbledon the dazzling Frenchwoman, Mlle. Suzanne Lenglen, Women's Champion of the World, retained her title against Miss Ryan of the U.S.A.

In the world of cricket, the first test match since 1912, played at Sydney in the winter of 1920, showed what the Australian eleven could do. Fit, strong, sun-soaked, the men who had fought alongside England in the war proceeded to demolish her neatly throughout the whole series, despite the presence of England's outstanding players, Hobbs, Hendren, Makepeace, and Hearne. When the Australians paid a return visit in 1921 the championship remained in Australian hands after three triumphant tests. Photographs of both elevens show the players to be curiously middle-aged and shabby-looking; they did not, we might think, see themselves as glamour figures or public entertainers.

Flying machines that were not bombers were seen in quantities in the air and presented no threat. In February 1919 the Air Ministry instituted a civil aviation department; and in a matter of weeks, after permission had been granted for commercial flying, the first British airline, Air Transport and Travel Ltd., was offering regular service to Paris. Restless young ex-officers like James Bellamy were experimenting with private machines, taking "hops" and "flips" across the Channel, at some risk to themselves and their passengers. Airliners replaced bombers after the firm of Handley Page converted a long-range night bomber into a passenger airship. It was expensive and ponderous to fly, but it could go anywhere up to 500 miles. Taking to the air was far from foolproof. In August 1921 the airship ZR2 (formerly R.38) crashed in flames into the River Humber during its trial trip before being handed over to America. It was the

A red-letter day for aviation: Independent companies flying between London and the Continent join to form the Imperial Air Transport Company.

The charabanc, a roomy motor coach, transportation for the lower classes

biggest airship in the world, a third as big again as the R.34, which had flown to America and back in 1919.

Britain's roads were even busier than her skies. William Morris and Henry Ford were fighting a price-reducing duel to catch the family-car buyer. It was 1922 before Sir Herbert Austin brought out his "Austin Seven," a small, square, ugly car that at first was thought to be slightly ridiculous but that was in fact the direct precursor of the "Mini" (the ubiquitous small car of today's England), and a realistic vehicle for increasingly crowded roads. (These roads were still as dusty or muddy as they had been when Dickens remarked on the "gritty" nastiness of London streets, for asphalt paving had not yet arrived.) Towering above the little "Seven" was the charabanc, a roomy motor coach that was to replace the train as a vehicle for getting to the country or the seaside when the Bellamys' servants took a day's outing.

For indoor pleasures the people of these early 1920s might go to "the pictures," probably to see an American film, for, after a rush of patriotic, spy, and news films early in the war, Britain's film industry had become relatively inactive. It was beginning to raise its head again at last, but the silver screen was still dominated by such thrilling dramas as those starring the romantic Douglas Fairbanks and his wife, Mary Pickford. Mary Pickford visited London in 1920 and was rapturously received. The next year an even warmer welcome was given to everybody's favourite, Charles Chaplin, who, people were surprised to see, was not a figure of fun but "a pleasant-faced, well-groomed and serious-minded young man anxious to be permitted to visit the scenes of his early days unaccompanied by a crowd. He found London changed; there was a sadness in it. In the old days it was more mysterious and romantic." Yet he said, "I love London more than ever. I love the whole feeling and atmosphere of it. It is a joy to me simply to know that this is London, and I am here. The streets seem more narrow than they were. It seems a more intimate city than it was. Perhaps it is a spiritual change. The people, too, seem so much nicer, so human."

A more surprising visitor to London arrived in May 1921. The Austrian Fritz Kreisler played the violin at the Queen's Hall. Three years earlier he had been fighting for the Emperor. At the Albert Hall Chaliapin was singing for the Russian Famine Fund, after a struggle with British authorities who feared the spread of Bolshevism to England through his visit.

Charles Chaplin in the film Shoulder Arms

The British people, anxiously trying to get homes together, to find jobs, or simply to be entertained, could not avoid knowing that the world was still in a sad state, even though Germany had been beaten. Nearby in Ireland there were battles between the Republicans and the Black and Tans, soldiers sent over from England to try to control the activities of the Irish nationalists, the Sinn Fein. Shootings, arson, and murders of policemen and civilians were the IRA's method of objecting to Britain's refusal to grant independence to all of Ireland. The death toll was mounting, foreshadowing similar tragedies of the Sixties and Seventies. At last, in July 1921, a truce was signed, and negotiations were begun in London between Republican leaders and the British government. At the opening of the Ulster Parliament the King and Queen had been present, and there was great pageantry and rejoicing. It seemed that things there, at least for the time being, were settled.

India, too, was clamouring for independence under the leadership of the peace-loving, ascetic Mahatma Gandhi, and Egypt was following suit. China was suffering terrible famine after the drought of 1920; children who could not be fed were sold or thrown into the river. Civil war was imminent and the way was being paved for radical change. The League of Nations was struggling to rehabilitate Austria, "the pauper State of Europe," and those who cast an eye on Germany noted that Adolf Hitler, discharged from the German Army, was making a name for himself as an orator in the National Socialist Workers' Party. Benito Mussolini, in Italy, had established *fasci*, or groups of workers, to press for social revolutionary change. In 1922 he marched on Rome and was invited by King Victor Emmanuel III to form a government. Signposts to the future were clearly marked to be seen by those with political vision and particularly by the pessimistic Mr. Hudson.

But, said the optimists, there could surely never be whole-scale war again when mass communications were growing at such a rate. In 1920 the Marconi Company opened the first British broadcasting station near Chelmsford in Essex, and the great Australian singer Dame Nellie Melba broadcast from it. Two years later a limited company was formed by a group of radio manufacturers to transmit from London with the call sign 2LO. The British Broadcasting Company had been born, and the miracle of radio was coming into first hundreds, then thousands of British homes by means of primitive little receiving sets that required the excited listeners to use headphones.

Edward enjoying the radio via a primitive receiving set

The early broadcasters performed under asylumlike conditions in studios resembling padded cells, with thick carpets and curtains and padded walls and ceilings. Singers and comedians were taken aback to find themselves without a visible, responsive audience in those little cells at Savoy Hill, London, where, from the windows of the BBC's offices, one looked out over the Embankment and across the Thames. In 1913 Walter Sickert had painted a picture called "Ennui," an all-too-vivid evocation of a suburban home: a man and woman utterly bored, she staring despairingly at a blank wall, he glazed-eyed over a glass of beer and a cigar. Domestic boredom on a scale impossible to conceive of in the late twentieth century must have been a constant guest in such homes— nothing to do, nothing to say. Never again would such boredom exist, for broadcasting brought a new form of entertainment, something that, at the adjustment of a "crystal" or "cat's whisker," came into the house like Shakespeare's Ariel with

> *. . . sounds and sweet airs*
> *That give delight, and hurt not.*

One of the many war memorials erected in the cities, towns, and villages across England

CHAPTER ELEVEN

Bright
Young Things
in the
Vortex

Whether or not Chaplin had been right about the *spiritual* change that he thought had come to London, a change there had certainly been. By 1922 the term "prewar" had come into the language; the war had marked a sharp break in everyone's life. Changes in the past, the deaths of Queen Victoria and of Edward VII that had closed previous eras, were insignificant compared with the change wrought by the Great War. Said Lord Carson, "There is nothing that England likes better than forgetting. It is easy to forget, particularly if it costs nothing." The Unknown Soldier lay buried in Westminster Abbey "in proud memory of those warriors who died unknown in the Great War," and architect Edwin Lutyens' cenotaph, the nation's war memorial, stood in Whitehall, visited yearly by the King on November 11, when two minutes' silence was respectfully and rigidly observed throughout the country in memory of the fallen dead. In every city, town, and village some form of war memorial had been erected, with its pathetic list of names in alphabetical order and its crowning figure of Victory or an armed soldier. Maimed men begged in the streets and unemployed ex-servicemen marched with posters protesting against their rejection. On Armistice Sunday church congregations sang Kipling's somber recessional: "Lord God of Hosts, be with us yet, Lest we forget—lest we forget!"

But people wanted to forget.

Were Londoners, as Chaplin felt, "so much nicer, so human"? Quite possibly, for war had eased class barriers and lessened prejudices as it always does and the expansion of the popular media brought increased knowledge and understanding of how the "other half" lived. Now parochialism and insularity were being broken down as people in Britain listened on their magical wireless sets to broadcasts from as far away as Paris and The Hague and watched films made in distant America. The publications of Northcliffe and Lord Beaverbrook and the popular magazines that were springing up were bringing people closer together. The "inalienable rights of man" had been talked about since the eighteenth century, but only now, at the beginning of the 1920s, were those rights being given practical expression by His Majesty's government. Housing, health, and education were all steadily improving. London was architecturally little changed from her Victorian self but was no longer the London in which Jack the Ripper had flourished or could have flourished. Slum clearance had begun long before the war, and building in central London was gradually replacing small old structures with grandiose new ones, such as Bush House on the curve of the Aldwych crescent, with its neo-Grecian frontage and huge classical sculptures. This was the last era in which London's buildings would be adorned with the great symbolical figures of deities, personifications of countries, and their attendant nymphs and cupids. When rebuilding began after the next war the human form would have vanished from architecture.

The ever-widening London streets still had some hansom cabs, but the motor buses on which Rose had been a conductorette during the war dominated the traffic lanes. Streetcars, a much slower means of transport, were far less dangerous to the pedestrian than the large vehicles of the rival omnibus companies, which, with motorcars, every year accounted for thousands of people killed and injured. They were not uniformly red, as are the London buses of today, but all colours, depending on the company owning them.

If London was changing, the surrounding countryside was becoming unrecognizable. Housing estates spread in every direction, swallowing up what had been semirural villages in Middlesex, Surrey, Essex, and Kent. Fields, country lanes, woods, streams, and wildlife disappeared under the handiwork of the speculative builder, whose aim was to throw up as many dwellings as possible, regardless of beauty. They were mainly built to the same design: semidetached, of brick often faced with stucco or imitation half-timbering in black and

FINEST VALUE IN METROLAND ! !
HARROW GARDEN VILLAGE

The ESTATE of OPEN SPACES and CHARMING COUNTRY HOUSES that are substantially built of all English materials. Brick with tiled roofs. Double slate damp courses.

Price £955 FREEHOLD. £45 TOTAL DEPOSIT. 28/6 per week NO Law Costs, NO Stamp Duties, NO Survey Fees, NO Extras

Advertisement for homes in one of the many housing estates

white—a style facetiously known as pseudo-Tudor. There would be a small garden at the front, a larger one at the back, a shed for Father's lawnmower and gardening tools. Inside there would probably be three bedrooms; a front living room, no longer known as the parlour but as the lounge; a smaller dining room at the back with, perhaps, French doors to the garden; and a solid-fuel boiler to heat the water. The bath in a separate room (now a compulsory feature) might well be the first the house owner or lessee had ever had, for the vast majority had been brought up in the tradition of taking a weekly bath in front of the kitchen fire in a tin slipper-bath that would, when not in use, be hung outside.

A novelty, too, would be the indoor toilet, which might be in the bathroom or separate. Earlier houses fortunate enough to contain either bath, toilet, or both would have sacrificed a bedroom for the purpose, as the Bellamys had done; otherwise a tin slipper-bath and a closet in the garden or yard would have to serve. The innovation was one of several that transformed life for dwellers in those uniform little houses in the ribbon developments, nearly every one of which would be dignified by a name as well as a street number. The smaller the house the more imposing the name—Balmoral, Sandringham, Bella Vista— and the name would sometimes tell a story comprehensible or otherwise to the passerby: Marysholme, Uanmee, Kozikott. Returned soldiers who had acquired a bit of French liked to call their houses Le Nid or Mon Repos. Comic or pretentious these names might be, but they were an attempt at individuality in areas where each house on a road might be the duplicate of its neighbours. The names were also an expression of pride in a new, clean, up-to-date home such as one's parents could never have imagined.

Edward and Daisy would have considered such a house pure luxury. It would not have occurred to them that future generations would look with distaste on the monotonous rows of buildings thrown up without regard for planning or the preservation of open spaces and on the dreary, uniform esplanades of shops that connected and served them.

The contents of the new homes were also inclined to lack beauty. Those who could afford to refurnish were getting rid of heavy Edwardian and Victorian furniture and replacing it with lighter modern pieces, mass-produced and characterless. Upholstery was usually of uncut *moquette*, giving the effect of very coarse velvet and patterned in the geometrical designs so much in style, usually in green and brown; cream paint for walls and woodwork was in favour. Carpets and curtains were equally ugly. Rooms without carpets had floor coverings of linoleum, washable but cheerless to the eye. The new system of hire purchase, known as the "Never-never" because payment by instalments seemed to the payer to be unending, tempted householders to buy furniture beyond their means and to crowd out their small rooms with it.

The new chain stores, particularly Woolworth's, whose motto was "Nothing over sixpence!" provided an amazing range of cheap goods. The factories were turning out cheap, badly finished ornaments, plaster dogs and children, vases and knickknacks, as tasteless as might be expected for the price. Antique objects often suffered the fate of old furniture, given to the garbage collector or to a

A typical living room in one of the new homes

charity sale, and were replaced with examples of Art Deco. A particular favourite was the Borzoi Girl, a streamlined young female with an unlikely torso and improbably long legs being dragged along, it appeared, by an equally stream-lined hound. (Fifty years later she would be much sought after by collectors.)

But not everything in the homes of the New Georgians was ugly. Children could play with toys more beautiful and intricate than any seen today. Germany, frantically trying to restore her economic balance, was exporting the lovely dolls for which she had long been famous. These dolls were elegant creations who might have composition bodies but whose faces would be of the most delicately tinted china, with long-fringed eyes that shut when the doll was laid down, or, following the Victorian tradition, the doll's body might be of sawdust-stuffed cotton with a bust, head, and forearms of wax and, of course, real hair. They made no attempt to be garishly modern, nor were they physically developed like this generation's "teenage" dolls. They were imaginatively conceived from a wide range of characters: fairy dolls wearing stiffened tutus of muslin, with a tinsel star on crown and wand; mermaids; gorgeous Indian princes in glittering costumes; tiny porcelain creatures the length of a finger joint dressed in perfect crocheted reproductions of the dress of George III's day.

The dolls' houses were usually reproductions of modern detached or semidetached homes, but the furniture and objects they contained were reproductions of antique furniture on a miniature scale, beautifully made, with accessories also to scale: exquisite tiny sets of tumblers and decanters, tea and dinner sets of egg-shell china, minute candelabra. Such things came from Czechoslovakia and Hungary, as yet undarkened by the Iron Curtain. The peak and perfection of all dolls' houses was the one presented to Queen Mary at the Wembley Exhibition of 1924. Designed by Sir Edwin Lutyens, the distinguished architect, it had been created by a conclave of artists and craftsmen and was a miracle of craftsmanship. A fairy palace, its library was stocked with 170 books whose contents were written in many cases by such authors as John Galsworthy, Rudyard Kipling, and Sir James Barrie in their own handwriting. Edmund Dulac, a famous artist and illustrator, had painted the nursery with pictures of fairy stories; reproductions of the Crown Jewels were contained in a strongroom; and the cellar was stocked with bottles of real wine and whisky. Nothing like it had ever been created before; an entire book was published about it. The house still exists, fortunately, in all its perfection and can be seen by visitors to Windsor Castle.

Alice, Virginia Bellamy's daughter by her first marriage, would be able to enjoy a great range of toys, but her brother William would be expected to confine himself to toy soldiers and the wind-up train set, with proper stations and signals that worked, which fascinated father as much as son. Boys of William's station in life were expected to follow "manly" pursuits from an early age, in preparation for the spartan boarding schools to which they would be sent at the age of eight or so.

Neither Alice nor William would be likely to follow the daily adventures of the cartoon character Teddy Tail and his friends, or those of Pip the dog, Squeak the penguin, and Wilfred the rabbit; the *Daily Mirror* picture paper and the *Daily Mail* would not penetrate to the upper regions of No. 165.

However, another cartoon character was a favorite with everyone, high or low. Early in the 1920s the American Pat Sullivan created Felix the Cat, who starred in an animated film series so popular that a cheer went up when the titles appeared on the cinema screen. Resourceful and resilient, Felix, obviously

Rose overseeing Alice's and William's studies

possessed of many more than the traditional feline nine lives, came through trial after trial, miraculously survived, and added a phrase to the language as he "kept on walking." In the words of his theme song, they "blew him up with dynamite but him they couldn't kill . . . he landed down in Timbuctoo and kept on walking still." Other cheerful ditties of the time, with more or less idiotic words, were "It Ain't Gonna Rain No Mo', No Mo'" and "Yes, We Have No Bananas." They were sung, whistled, and hummed everywhere, for the wireless spread popular music farther than it had ever been spread before. In the 1890s nobody in Northumberland would be likely to have heard of Lottie Collins' ballad "Ta-ra-ra-boom-de-ay," then being performed in a London music hall; in 1923 and thereafter all Britain was aware of the latest hit in the rising industry that would one day be given the blanket name of "Pop."

In 1920 the first electrically recorded gramophone discs were produced, and every house that could afford it had a gramophone, adorned with the familiar label of the dog listening to His Master's Voice. Classical music was becoming known to people who had never been to a concert in their lives; taste and appreciation were growing. By 1923 almost half a million held wireless licences (and thousands more listened in without them). News, talks, the Children's Hour with its "Aunts" and "Uncles," religion, and music were available from the BBC. Enthusiasts for regionalism might complain that the standard BBC voice was ousting the good old native accents, but in fact the influence of the early announcers helped to iron out sloppy speech and vocal ugliness as parents urged their children to "talk proper, like the wireless." Announcers, elegant though unseen in immaculate evening dress, had something of the status of today's pop stars without the demonstrations; they were revered, godlike Voices. The public loved nothing more than to hear one of its idols make a gaffe, as when the "golden voice" of Stuart Hibberd was heard to announce that a concert would be heard from the Bathroom at Pump (instead of the Pumproom at Bath).

Funny stories and cartoons abounded. *Punch* showed the frenzied agony of "expert heckler on hearing vulnerable arguments in electioneering speech." *The Sketch* portrayed a Wireless Widow sadly knitting while her husband sat with his back to her, earphones clamped to his head. Even hair fashions followed the new craze. In 1923 those young women whose hair was long enough wore it in

A familiar label, showing the faithful dog listening to "His Master's Voice"

Sybil Thorndike as St. Joan

the "earphone" style, parted in the centre with a plait on each side coiled up over the ears.

In spite of the lure of the receiving set, people read more than they had ever done. It was a vintage time for authors. Shaw had a host of great plays behind him before the production in 1923 of the one that would live as his strongest dramatic work, *St. Joan*. The young Sybil Thorndike proved to be the ideal Joan, sturdy, colloquial, yet transformed in her great moments into a being inspired. Shaw had been unpopular during the war years for his pacifist views, which some had described as downright treasonous, but *Joan* regained him esteem. D. H. Lawrence had written *Women in Love* in 1920 and *Aaron's Rod* in 1922, the year in which H. G. Wells published his *Short History of the World* and A. S. M. Hutchinson produced a best-selling novel, *If Winter Comes*. The master storyteller W. Somerset Maugham was writing plays shrewdly reflecting the times he lived in, and the American-born poet T. S. Eliot wrote his pessimistic masterpiece *The Waste Land* in 1922. On a lower but livelier plane, England was revelling in the immortally funny stories of P. G. Wodehouse. His perfect valet, Jeeves (who "oiled" or "oozed" into a room rather than entering it in the usual manner), his brainless though amiable man-about-town, Bertie Wooster, the incompetent Ukridge, the troops of frivolous girls and dragonish aunts who beset his heroes, though highly topical, managed to transcend mere topicality; whereas Michael Arlen's highly successful novel *The Green Hat*, a *genre* work set in the Mayfair in which Wodehouse's comics moved, lived on only as a period piece.

Women writers had come into their own as something rather more respected than Gilbert's "lady novelist who never would be missed," gibed at in *The Mikado*. The romantic novel had risen from being merely one of the "storyettes" with which Rose or Mrs. Bridges would pass the time after supper. Women were writing for a mass audience of their own, library borrowers and book buyers who, after the horrors of war, longed for escapist romance. Many of these women readers were bereaved and lonely, only too aware that their chances for marriage were slender, with so many men of their generation buried in France and Flanders. If vicarious romance could be had between the covers of a book, they were ready for it. No plot could be too improbable, no love story too passionate (though only in a nice way, for sex as such had not reared its ugly head to any height). They wanted sentiment, tears, thrills, hearts and flowers, moonlight and roses, and they got them from Ethel M. Dell, Elinor Glyn, Ruby M. Ayres, May Sinclair, and Berta Ruck, among others. They all specialized in stern young heroes with jutting jaws and strong arms ready to whisk up the frail little woman at a moment's notice and press burning lips to hers. More literary were Tennyson Jesse, Sheila Kaye-Smith of the earthy Sussex novels, Clemence Dane, and the brilliant Rebecca West.

For men who wanted lightish fare there were the "rattling good yarns" of Edgar Wallace, "Sapper" (H.C. McNeile), and the manly tales of another ex-serviceman, "Ian Hay" (Major Ian Hay Beith). Writers varying from the excellent to the mediocre abounded, for never had there been so many outlets for fiction, humourous articles, essays, and poetry than at this peak time for magazines and periodicals of all kinds.

Films, too, were booming. Chaplin was the admitted King of the Comics (though he wisely included a touch of Little Man pathos in everything he did), but he was run a close second by the deadpan slapstick master Buster Keaton and the spectacled Harold Lloyd, who in spite of his diffident appearance performed the most extraordinary acrobatic feats of stunt work, reaching a climax in *Safety Last*. Romantic heroes abounded, the most famous being the superbly hand-

Buster Keaton keeps a steady watch in The Navigator, *while Harold Lloyd hangs from one in* Safety Last.

some young Italian who called himself Rudolph Valentino. He had first been noticed by the public in *The Four Horsemen of the Apocalypse* in 1921, following it up by conquering female hearts with *The Sheik, Blood and Sand*, and *The Son of the Sheik*. He was, to romance-starved women, the living equivalent of the love-story hero. Even today, when the great seduction scenes and purple passages of his films seem ludicrous, his own star quality and peculiar charm shine through

Rudolph Valentino and Agnes Ayres in The Sheik

and make clear what an amazing impact he must have had on the cinemagoers of his time.

Vilma Banky and Pola Negri were among the leading film "vamps" of the day, sinuously sexy in overwhelming make-up, slinky satin, and galaxies of stage jewels; and heroines were the perennial favorite Mary Pickford, the beautiful sisters Gish, Gloria Swanson, and in England Betty Balfour as the cheeky Cockney "Squibs." The servants at No. 165 would have no difficulty in finding films to go to on their nights off.

In the theatre the versatile, witty young Noel Coward was not only rising in his profession but becoming a symbol of one aspect of his generation. His comedy *The Young Idea*, produced at the Savoy Theatre in 1923, brought a breath of fresh air into the lives of playgoers. Immediately afterwards he went into André Charlot's revue *London Calling*, of which he was part author. Then, in the following year, he appeared in his own play *The Vortex*, playing Nicky Lancaster, a fast-living young man who had a slightly ambiguous relationship with his mother and who took "snow," powdered cocaine, the fashionable drug of the time. The combination of drugs, adultery, and hinted incest was an immediate *succès de scandale*. The more critics condemned it as immoral the more the public flocked to it. Young Noel Coward, in his near-uniform of silk dressing gown, casual ascot, and brilliantined hair, became the emblem of the "Younger Generation knock-knock-knocking at the door," in his words. He was decadent, delicious; he stood for the Bright Young Things.

The Bright Young Things were the inevitable result of the war. Some had been involved in it, like Georgina; others were too young. They were rich, or their parents were; they did no work and lived for pleasure. The girls were "flappers" who wore boyish tubular dresses, shortened their skirts, smoked

Young Noel Coward: "He was decadent, delicious; he stood for the Bright Young Things."

James Bellamy and Polly Merivale in typical flapper garb

cigarettes, preferably scented or Turkish, in long holders, after the fashion popularized by Coward, and who rode on the pillions of their boy friends' motor bikes, wearing bright red lipstick, powder, and rouge. Their escorts were on the lines of Wodehouse's Bertie Wooster of the Drones Club, long, languid young men with pencil moustaches, fashionable baggy trousers, sporty blazers, and pronounced drawls. They called each other Old Thing and Old Horse (irrespective of sex), expressed approval by "ripping," "topping," "deevy," "too too," and disapproval by "utterly foul," "dashed bad form," and the like. They were always either giving or going to parties: fancy-dress parties, bottle parties, masked parties, parties verging on the orgiastic, and, particularly, cocktail parties.

The first cocktail known to history was described in an American periodical of 1816, and the first British cocktail bar was opened in London by the great chef

Parties, parties, parties: They were the order of the day.

A costumed partygoer takes a spill.

Alexis Soyer in 1851. It lasted five months before being closed down as a danger to morals. Thereafter the cocktail remained in abeyance for half a century. Even the aperitif, familiar, even indispensable to us, was not a feature of the late Victorian and Edwardian dinner party. The pre-dinner drink simply did not exist, except surreptitiously. Sherry might be drunk with the soup, but that was the earliest. Dinner, even with Queen Victoria, had to be embarked upon cold sober. Only in the postwar years did the aperitif, or cocktail, come into its own. The Manhattan, Sidecar, White Lady, Martini were not only drunk before dinner as an appetizer or warmer-up, but whole parties were devoted to their consumption, together with canapés. (One noted member of the aristocracy wound up in court for a breach of the peace in connection with a party at which the guests all dressed as babies, pushing each other in perambulators and carts.) Waiters in hotel bars had to become accomplished in shaking the concoctions in a metal flask with crushed ice. The more affluent dwelling house boasted a cocktail cabinet, specially designed to hold the ingredients and glasses for mixing cocktails; these still survive, some models even being so designed as to light up and play a tune.

Music was provided by jazz combinations, but for private entertainment the "in" thing was played—the ukulele, a four-stringed guitar-type instrument that had started life in Portugal and had become popular in Hawaii and the United States. Its plaintive plink-plonk was to be heard up and down Britain (for its popularity knew no class barriers), and special songs, notably "Ukulele Lady," were written for it.

Night clubs and cabarets flourished. The Trocadero, the Criterion, the Piccadilly Hotel, the Metropole with "Midnight Follies" were only a few catering to the all-night clientele. They were the neo-Georgian equivalents of those Victorian establishments to which young bloods, Bohemians, and literary men used to repair—Kate Hamilton's, the Cyder Cellars, the early music halls—with the enormous difference that the new night haunts were open to both sexes. The "flappers" now had the vote, like their elder sisters. In contrast with the recent events in Russia, this small but significant development was a sign of the great, bloodless social revolution that would gather pace in England as the twentieth century advanced.

The doors of the Fourth Shrine of Tutankhamen's tomb

CHAPTER TWELVE

Singing the Blues

Unemployment might be steadily rising and the gigantic national debt causing concern, but there were plenty of other topics for both Upstairs and Downstairs to discuss in the years between 1924 and 1926. One was the recent discovery at Luxor in Upper Egypt of the tomb of the boy king Tutankhamen (the name received various spellings and pronunciations and was popularly shortened to King Tut). It was exciting to archaeologists all over the world, for the work of the ancient tomb robbers in the pyramids their builders had thought impregnable had been extremely thorough. Even when the building of pyramids was abandoned and the royal tombs were made in the rock face of the Nile cliffs, the spoilation went on. Apparently, not one tomb had been left unrifled.

But Tutankhamen had been lucky. He was a rather unimportant pharaoh, who had become one only through his marriage. Crowned at twelve, he was dead by the age of eighteen or thereabouts and was buried in a comparatively modest tomb.

Two hundred years later, when the tomb of Rameses VI was being built, above that of Tutankhamen, the workmen threw down piles of limestone rubble that built up a complete rampart covering the entrance to the boy king's tomb from all eyes. Thus it came about that the first eyes to see it, nearly 3,000 years later, were British. The fifth Earl of Carnarvon had been making significant discoveries in Thebes since 1906, with a break during the war, in association with the Egyptologist Howard Carter, Inspector General to the Antiquities Department of the Egyptian Government. On February 16, 1923, their expedition broke through to the sepulchral chamber of Tutankhamen. Less than two months later Lord Carnarvon's dramatically sudden death at the tomb entrance started the legend that all London was soon talking about: the Curse of the Pharaohs. As time went on story after story was told of the fatal accidents and misfortunes that befell those who despoiled a royal tomb of Egypt; nevertheless, Howard Carter survived to reveal glory after glory as the exploration progressed, and on January 24, 1924, he penetrated the tomb chamber itself.

Through the newspapers, reports came back to England of the tomb's wonders. There was the huge stone sarcophagus which held the young king's mummy, intact enough for examination to show that he had probably died from natural causes. His tomb furniture was of an unbelievable richness and beauty. Gold, silver, alabaster, magnificent lionesses of red granite, two crowned figures of gods of the Nile, state chariots as freshly gilded as when they had been placed in the tomb for the benefit of the occupant's spirit, paintings showing the king in his lifetime—the treasures were endless, beyond legend. A wave of Egyptomania swept England, as it had done after Nelson's victory at the Battle of the Nile. Sphinxes, sacred cats, scarabs, Egyptian fashions, and Egyptian jewellery were the rage. "King Tut" was the subject of revue sketches and cartoons. Interest revived in long-forgotten figures from Egypt's history: the beautiful Queen Nefertiti, whose long-necked head in reproduced sculpture or in paintings was a fashionable decoration of the time, and her husband Ikhnaton; they had been Tutankhamen's parents-in-law. And, long after the mania had faded, Howard Carter lived on despite the "Curse," dying in 1939 at the age of sixty-six.

Other wonders were nearer home. The British Empire, long revered as a tower of strength by both Britain and those countries who flew her flag, was celebrated in 1924 by a magnificent tribute that took two years to create and cost more than ten million pounds. At the beginning of the century the Middlesex village of Wembley had been a modest place known only for its park. In 1924 it became the site of the British Empire Exhibition, a mammoth project that drew visitors from all over the world. Its purpose was to show the range of the Empire's power and wealth and to exhibit her products. Opening it on St. George's Day, April 23, King George (who was of course also Emperor) said that the Exhibition might be said "to reveal to us the whole Empire in little, containing within its 220 acres of ground a vivid model of the architecture, art, and industry of all the races which come under the British flag . . . we believe that this Exhibition will bring the peoples of the Empire to a better knowledge of how to meet their reciprocal wants and aspirations."

His words were heard all over Britain, broadcast through a microphone suspended above his head. For the first time the British people heard their monarch's voice broadcast, and there can have been little work done that day when the historic speech was made.

That was Exhibition Summer, on an immensely greater scale than the summer of 1851 when the Crystal Palace had been London's pride and joy and great tourist attraction. It was hard for visitors to know what to see first. Mrs. Bridges, accompanied by Mr. Hudson, always avid for culture, would have been torn between a stroll in the gardens, bright with tulips and delphiniums, a visit to a reconstruction of Tutankhamen's tomb, the Palace of Arts, to which the King among others had lent art treasures, or the Indian Pavilion with its bewilderingly beautiful carpets, silks, materials interwoven with glittering tinsel thread, many-armed gods and goddesses, and lovely young tawny-skinned Indian women wrapped in graceful saris with caste jewels in their foreheads and noses.

Daisy and Edward certainly made for the amusement park, which offered a vast range of entertainment, including a boating lake and a scenic railway. Virginia's son William and a host of boys of all ages would be enthralled by the Palace of Engineering and the real coal mine that one could descend in a cage. Children found an exciting blend of terror and enjoyment in the "Derby Racer" and the "Jack and Jill," a mechanical car that carried its brave passengers to the top of a tower, at which point the bottom fell out and they descended, shrieking, on slides. Children without the requisite nerve for that could be photographed with an effigy of Felix the Cat or buy a delicious-smelling oiled silk parasol from a smiling Singhalese or travel on the scenic railway; Queen Mary herself graciously condescended to do this on a private visit.

One thing no visitor would miss seeing was in the Canadian Pavilion—a statue of the Prince of Wales in butter. The hard-working King and Queen were popular, but the Prince was idolized. Perpetually boyish in looks, though now aged thirty, he had been in the public eye since his early childhood. There was a strong element of the playboy in his character; had he been situated as his grandfather Edward VII was for so many years he might well have given himself

The Prince of Wales attending the British Legion Rally at the Crystal Palace

over to amusement. But his sense of duty was stronger. Naturally shy, he forced himself to meet all classes and types of people, to open endless exhibitions and appear in public to such a degree that his solitary pursuit of flying must have been a joy in removing him temporarily from human contact.

His insistence on going to France when war broke out won him immense admiration. When Lord Kitchener protested at his exposing himself to danger, he replied that he was not irreplaceable because he had four younger brothers. Kitchener is said to have retorted, "If I were certain you would be shot, I do not know that I should be right to restrain you. What I cannot permit is the chance, which exists till we have a settled line, of the enemy securing you as a prisoner." But by November 1914 the Prince was in France. He served on the Western

Front with the Expeditionary Force and in various other capacities throughout the war, always good-humoured and democratic, as ready to share a packet of cigarettes or play football with ordinary Tommies as to journey out to Egypt or the Italian front. He was serving with the Canadian force at the time of the Armistice—hence the statue.

After the war he referred to his part in it as "insignificant," an opinion shared by nobody else. No sooner was he back in England than he was involved in a whirl of duties, going down a tin mine, investigating slum conditions in the East End of London, visiting the shipyards of the Clyde, before setting off on the first of the tours that would take him all over the Empire and twice to the United States. His affability and modesty endeared him wherever he went; his smile was the most famous in the world. At times his right hand would become useless from perpetual handshaking, and his light tenor voice would be reduced to a whisper. (The author's father, on being introduced to him, noted with compassion the Prince's painful blush, a sign of the strain of meeting yet another stranger.) Who could grudge him his flying, his golf, and his dancing? He was doing more for his country than any royal personage had done before, as ambassador and worker. He was not only the darling of the people but their white hope, the young man back from the war who was to build a better Britain. None among the multitudes who cheered him could have guessed that the time would come when he would sadly retire from kingship into exile, unable to face life without the woman he loved, whom his government and church thought unsuitable to be a queen.

A year before the opening of the Wembley Exhibition the Prince of Wales' brother, Albert, Duke of York, had married a very pretty Scots girl, the dark-haired, blue-eyed Lady Elizabeth Bowes-Lyon. Three years later the announcement in the Bellamys' copy of *Country Life* of the birth of Princess Elizabeth caused no great stir, only congratulations. At the time none would have dreamed that, one day in distant 1952, the baby would, by reason of King Edward VIII's resignation of his crown to his brother, her father, become Queen Elizabeth II. The pretty Duchess of York would at the same time become the beloved Queen Mother, even more beautiful and charming in her later years than as a bride.

The baby Elizabeth, or "Lillibet," as her family called her, probably had in her nursery bookcase those children's books that had just begun to enrapture England, *When We Were Very Young* and *Winnie the Pooh*. A. A. Milne, novelist

*Albert and Elizabeth,
the Duke and Duchess
of York, leaving
London for their
honeymoon*

Princess Elizabeth in her pram accompanied by her grandfather, King George V

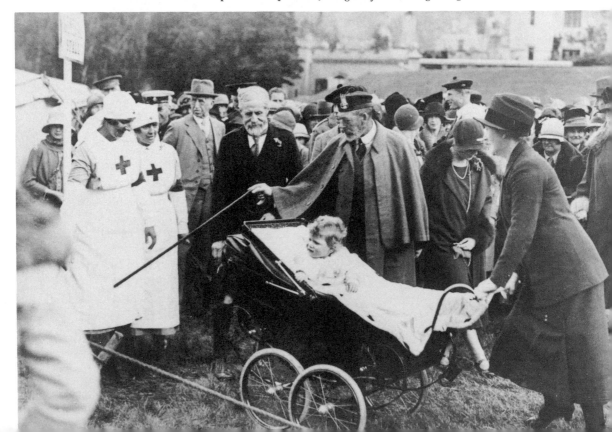

and playwright, had begun to write poems and stories around the personality of his small son, Christopher Robin, and his toys, Pooh Bear, the Strange and Bouncy Tigger, Piglet, Rabbit, Kanga, and her baby Roo. They were peculiarly English, distinctly upper-class; Christopher Robin had a nursemaid, Alice, with whom on a celebrated occasion he went to Buckingham Palace, and a nanny, whose dressing gown was "a beautiful blue, but it hadn't a hood," as Christopher Robin observed while saying his prayers. Kensington Gardens were the familiar haunt of such nannies and their charges and would be for many years to come.

While London's children of the rich fed the ducks on the Round Pond, were wheeled in their perambulators, or were shown the fairy-wreathed statue of Peter Pan, their young parents danced. The year 1923 saw the emergence of a new rhythm, the blues, and a new sort of singer, the "whispering baritone," whose husky crooning was considered most alluring. The blues were news, with their suggestion of romantic melancholia and mild decadence. Quite a new kind of show hit London in the year of their birth, *You'd Be Surprised*, a "jazzaganza." It

Christopher Robin with his friends: Kanga, Roo, Owl, Piglet, Pooh, and Rabbit

Learning the Charleston

was a strange blend of the newest jazz and classical numbers, including a ballet by Darius Milhaud, danced by the young Ninette de Valois. In the same year came something that was to become itself a classic: George Gershwin's *Rhapsody in Blue*, performed at the Aeolian Hall, New York. "Blue" was the word of the moment, rhyming, of course, with "you" and "true." The Bright Young Things were dancing the Charleston, which had crossed the Atlantic to storm England. Popular opinion at first condemned its knee-knocking antics as "vulgar," and a vicar proclaimed, "It's neurotic! It is rotten! It stinks! Phew, open the windows!" Songs tended to follow the blue line: "What'll I Do?," "All Alone" (by the Telephone), and "Among My Souvenirs."

But the London theatre was cheerful enough: *The Beggar's Opera* was still running at the Lyric in 1923, delighting audiences with pretty Queen Anne costumes in the formalized production of Nigel Playfair, and at the Aldwych the famous Aldwych farces had begun, starring the rakish Tom Walls and the silly-ass, dude-type Ralph Lynn, with the gentle, ineffectual, bald Robertson Hare always getting mistaken for somebody else, coming in at the wrong moment, or losing his trousers. In 1925 the handsome American John Barrymore was playing Hamlet at the Haymarket, *Rose Marie* at Drury Lane was producing a widespread case of "Indian Love Call" on the brain, and *No, No, Nanette* at the Palace was embarrassing Queen Mary with the scantiness of its chorus's bathing costumes.

In 1925 cinemagoers were thrilled by a visit to London from the most adored of film stars. Rudolph Valentino arrived in person to attend the premiere of his film *The Eagle*. A wild reception greeted him. His adorers were all the more shocked when, a year later, he died suddenly and dramatically, aged only 31. His funeral was attended by thousands of weeping women and filmed by newsreel cameras.

"The Deep Blue Sea" number from No, No, Nanette

Three hairstyles from which the fashionable young woman could choose

A shocking exhibition of knees

The girls who mourned Valentino were very different in appearance from those who had swooned over him in *The Four Horsemen of the Apocalypse* in 1921. Their hair was short, bobbed like Sybil Thorndike's in *St. Joan*, shingled, the back cut short with clippers like a man's, or clipped in a squarer style. Some went so far as to have the completely mannish Eton Crop. Their narrow skirts had risen to just below the knee in 1925, and by the next year female knees were on exhibition for the first time in Western history. They were making their own dresses on sewing machines, from "ready-made" patterns; their stockings were of flesh-coloured silk for the moneyed and artificial silk for the less well-off. Cloche hats, like upturned flowerpots, obscured the hair and half the face, wrap-round coats had heavy collars of fur, shoes had ankle straps and buttons, and "Russian boots" reaching about halfway up the calf enjoyed a brief vogue.

Young men in the fashion parade

Fashionable young men were at last breaking away from the dark-suit image with plus fours (cut like Elizabethan breeches), "Oxford bags," immensely wide cuffed trousers, sports jackets, and Fair Isle knitted pullovers.

A much greater change was taking place. In the nineteenth century Annie Besant had tried, against heavy odds, to spread the doctrine of birth control, which had been for so long a forbidden topic. In 1923 Dr. Marie Stopes revived the subject, urging couples to have fewer children and describing the techniques in books, such as *Married Love*, which caused a sensation. Her birth-control clinic in London attracted thousands of requests from women who thought that contraception and abortion were the same thing and wanted the latter. In spite of opposition and an unsuccessful libel action, her message got through; slowly people began to learn how not to have unwanted children.

Marie Stopes was, in the fashionable word, "sensational," as were many other items in the news. Mr. Hudson might not approve of the lurid details published in the newspapers of the 1920s, but readers devoured them. Crimes abounded, particularly murders that would come to be regarded as classic cases. In 1922 Edith Thompson was walking home with her husband from Ilford railway station in Essex when a young man ran up to them and stabbed Thompson fatally. He was Frederick Bywaters, a ship's steward, who had at one time been their lodger and had become Edith Thompson's lover. When he was away at sea they had exchanged passionate letters in which she had told Bywaters about her attempts to poison her husband by giving him powdered glass. The prosecution alleged that although she had not technically murdered Thompson she was guilty in that she had urged the impressionable, twenty-year-old Bywaters to do so. It seems very probable, on later study of the case, that the letters had been merely fantasies arising from a violently romantic nature and that she had made no attempts on her husband's life at all.

The jury decided, however, that her guilt was undeniable, and she was condemned to death. The hanging of women has always been a highly emotive business, and no woman had been hanged for fifteen years. General horror was felt at the verdict, but in spite of public and private protests Edith Thompson was dragged, literally, to the scaffold in a state of hysterical terror. Today, her trial reads as a miscarriage of justice.

The Armstrong case, in the same year, aroused great interest if less emotion. Enquiries into the life of a solicitor, Major Armstrong, led to the exhumation of his wife's body. It was found to contain arsenic, and Armstrong was hanged.

Mrs. Annie Besant

The case gave rise to a flood of detective stories which were already much in vogue since the appearance of Agatha Christie on the literary scene.

In 1924 one of the most gruesome murders of the decade was committed at a peaceful spot on the Sussex coast, in a bungalow at the Crumbles, near Pevensey. Patrick Mahon, an ex-convict with an unsavoury record, had rented the bungalow in order to entertain Emily Kaye, a woman older than himself with whom he was having an affair. He was tired of her and had gone through most of her money. They spent a few days together; then Emily Kaye disappeared. The following weekend Mahon took another young woman to the bungalow. Ignorance was bliss; she arrived and departed without knowing that Mahon had murdered Miss Kaye, cut up the body, burnt the head on the sitting-room fire, broken up the bones and strewn them around the garden, disposing of further bits of the corpse out of a train window on his way to London.

A suitcase, left at a London station, betrayed him. The judge gave no credence to Mahon's story that Emily Kaye had died by hitting her head on the coal scuttle, particularly as Mahon was known to have bought a cook's knife and a saw the day before going down to the bungalow. Mahon was hanged, and thousands of people who had devoured the ghastly details of the crime made ghoulish expeditions to the Crumbles, paying a shilling to go inside and inspect the scene of the murder.

Children gathering coal during the coal strike

The same morbid interest was taken after the hanging of another Sussex murderer, John Thorne, whose fiancée, Elsie Cameron, was found murdered and dismembered in the chicken run at Wesley Farm, Crowborough. The site was an irresistible attraction to souvenir hunters.

Such lurid cases as these enlivened the breakfast tables of Britain in company with news items less bloodcurdling but very ominous. Britain's export market was collapsing. Unemployment figures were rising, industrial disputes and strikes were rife (even policemen had struck for union recognition in 1919), but nowhere was there so much unrest as in the most essential industry—coal mining. Miners felt themselves to be vastly underpaid for the dirty, unpleasant job they did, particularly in the boom period after the war. When it collapsed in 1921 they were the hardest hit of all workers, and they went on strike. Public sympathy was not with them, for the fear of Communism was strong and the trades-union leaders were widely thought to be "Bolshies." That particular strike was quashed because Ernest Bevin, leader of the dockers, and J. H.

Thomas, the railwaymen's leader, refused to support the miners. For three months they fought on alone for more money, only to finish up with lower wages than ever.

By 1925 the coal industry was losing a million pounds a month, and pits were closing at a rapid rate. Unemployment rose, and conditions in the mining towns and villages of the north of England and Wales were acutely distressed. The mine owners' answer was to declare wage cuts unless the men were prepared to return to working an eight-hour day. This the Miners' Federation of Great Britain refused to accept and enlisted the help of the Trades Union Congress. Alarmed, Stanley Baldwin's Conservative government offered a temporary subsidy, and a royal commission was set up to investigate the industry's problems.

Women volunteers assisting with the mail during the general strike

In March 1926 its findings were published. The nationalization that the miners had called for was rejected, and the commission's constructive suggestions were impracticable at the time. All the Samuel Report held out to the virtually starving men was a 13½ percent pay cut. Understandably, the secretary of the Miners' Federation, the uncompromising A. J. Cook, smartly turned down the idea of smaller wages and longer hours. "Not a penny off the pay, not a second on the day," he said and was much quoted.

At the end of April the unions gave the TUC full powers to negotiate with the government or call a general strike. The Socialist Ramsay MacDonald warned against this "clumsy and ineffectual" weapon, which had no goal that might be regarded as victory. He proved to be utterly right.

The forces of the TUC were not organized; those of the government were. By the time the strike began, on May 3, a state of emergency had been declared with troops at the ready at key points. The strikers had paralyzed coal production, transport, food delivery, dock work, and a large part of the printing industry, but there was nothing they could actively do except watch other people take over these jobs and do them, on the whole, very competently. It was very much a class struggle. The household at No. 165 Eaton Place represented fairly enough the generally unsympathetic attitude of Britain in general, and in particular southern England, to the strikers. Communications were immeasurably better than they had ever been, but even so the southern suburbanites and the West End fashionables had no real idea of the plight of the miners. They had not seen and could not imagine the filthy, sweaty underground toil in primitive conditions, the ever-present risk of fatal disasters, the high incidence of the lung disease silicosis, caused by coal dust, or the plight of families living on next to nothing (perhaps on the few shillings an unemployed father had earned by scraping coal off a slag heap and selling it). To know all is to understand all, says the French proverb, and because they knew nothing they could not possibly understand.

Mr. Hudson felt ashamed of his "fellow workers," as he termed the strikers, and spoke strongly against the "forces of evil out to destroy our liberty." He volunteered at once to become one of London's 40,000 special constables, a duty he had enjoyed during the war. James Bellamy thought the strike intolerable and predicted mass violence. "It's been coming since the end of the war, only people have shut their eyes to it. What happened in Russia's going to happen here." He was one of those volunteers known as "the plus-fours brigade" who

Volunteers unloading milk during the general strike

undertook to drive a London bus. Others drove trams, even trains. Lorries containing food supplies were guarded by military convoys, and the Organization for the Maintenance of Supplies set up a food centre in Hyde Parke, manned by many titled people, who were photographed peeling potatoes and frying sausages. Edward collected milk from the Hyde Park Depot and displayed a sign in the front of the Bellamy car offering a lift to anyone who might need one.

Like the war, the strike brought Londoners closer together; there was a general air of cheerfulness as office workers travelled by brewer's dray or motor launch. Most theatres stayed open. Young women like Georgina continued to go to night clubs, and sporting events were as well patronized as ever. Those strikers who, like Ruby's Uncle Len from Barnsley, Yorkshire, had come to London as pit delegates to a strikers' meeting could see very little result for their

James driving a bus during the general strike

efforts, though clashes were taking place at bus depots, volunteer transport was threatened, and there were ugly incidents all over the country, including the derailing by strikers of the famous express train The Flying Scotsman. Newspapers might have been stopped, but from the third day of the strike the government was publishing its own daily newspaper, the *British Gazette*, edited by Winston Churchill on heavily propagandist lines. The BBC broadcast reports of the situation with fine impartiality, though its chairman, John Reith, refused to allow the Archbishop of Canterbury to broadcast an appeal for peace. Stanley Baldwin was heard over the air pointing out the threat the strike offered to constitutional liberty. The TUC issued a rival newspaper to the *British Gazette*, its own *British Worker*, but it is very doubtful whether it was read by many people other than those who already supported the strike.

Baldwin conveyed in his broadcasts that he would personally be responsible for seeing that the miners got their rights if the TUC would call off the strike, though the government would not negotiate terms. The TUC was not, and never had been, wholeheartedly in favour of the strike. Ernest Bevin and J. H. Thomas were moderates who feared that if it succeeded and extremists came into power they might find themselves with a national revolution on their hands. On May 12, nine days after the strike had begun, the general council went to 10 Downing Street to call it off.

And after all, there were no assurances that justice would be done, as Baldwin had intimated. Miners drifting back to work found themselves forced to accept a lower wage. For another seven months the rest held out before capitulating. The expensive, pointless, time-wasting general strike was over. Life would be back to normal in the Bellamy household and in the homes of those to whom it had been a novel, amusing interlude. For the miners, the struggle would go on.

The hood of a bus wired closed to prevent strikers from disabling the engine

First Theatre Audience
to See Television

To be shown on a Screen at

THE LONDON COLISEUM
on Monday, 28th July

S IR OSWALD STOLL, who has always been such a staunch
supporter of Britain and of everything British, has arranged
with the Baird Company to allot a part of the programme at

Announcement of the first theatre presentation of the marvel, television

Television's inventor, John Baird

CHAPTER THIRTEEN

Death
of a Decade

What was left of the Twenties would see an ever-accelerating pace of life and developments in scientific progress that would have gladdened the heart of Albert, Prince Consort. If the world had been shrinking before, now it was as though a magic wand were reducing it, like Cinderella's coach, to the size of a pumpkin. Many years before, a *Punch* artist had drawn a fanciful picture of a drawing room full of Victorians seated sedately round the fire, listening, by means of complicated apparatus, to a concert which they were also watching on a small screen. It must have caused great amusement at the time. The artist was a better prophet then he knew. In January 1926 the Scots-born John Logie Baird, who had been working on an invention for four years, demonstrated it in a room in London's Soho. It was the first showing of television. The next year, in Glasgow, he experimented with colour, and in 1929 the newspaper *The People* printed a report from a correspondent:

I have just witnessed in the Long Acre studios of Baird Television Development Company a demonstration of the most advanced wireless projection of moving pictures that the world has yet known. In the lens, or glass screen, of the receiving apparatus I could see clearly and vividly the three artistes whose voices came to me simultaneously with their visible movements and expressions. Having followed the progress of Mr.

Amelia Earhart, after her 1928 transatlantic flight

"Amy, Wonderful Amy" Johnson

Baird's wonderful invention, I am in a position to state that projections have enormously improved even within the past few weeks. Today the time has come when every holder of a wireless licence should be given the fullest possible opportunity of judging television for himself or herself.

In the previous year Baird had brought off a sensational coup by transmitting pictures across the Atlantic to an awed audience of four people. Techniques were improving, but it would be a long time before the *Punch* artist's vision was fulfilled and television came into the home. The first public television service, from Alexandra Palace in North London, could only be watched, in eye-straining conditions on a very small screen, by viewers within thirty-five miles of London, and families such as the Bellamys would be likely to regard it as a passing craze.

Britain and the United States were in closer contact than could have been conceived in the days when a ten-day voyage had been considered good going. The year 1927 saw the beginning of radio-telephone communication between the two countries and the first solo flight across the Atlantic by Charles Lindbergh. In 1928 the American Amelia Earhart became the first woman to make the flight. Amy Johnson outdid her in 1929, when she made history by flying solo from Croydon, England, to Australia in nineteen and a half days and became a national heroine, the first aviator to inspire a popular song ("Amy, Wonderful Amy"). Her feat was even more of a sensation than the first flight to the North Pole made by the American naval officer Richard E. Byrd. Sir Alan Cobham's long-distance flights prepared the flight paths for commercial companies, and with the production of the "Moth" in 1925 it became possible for an air enthusiast of moderate means to own his own plane. It was small, had a top speed of 90 mph, and, most conveniently, could be housed in a garage. In 1927, significantly, Britain won the coveted Schneider Trophy, awarded the winner of the international race for seaplanes.

The cinema, too, was leaping ahead. There had been crude early sound films before the war and experiments by a small company after it, but it was 1928 before Britain saw and heard the first successful talking feature film, *The Jazz Singer*, starring Al Jolson. It was followed up by an even greater box-office draw, *The Singing Fool*. The technique in these early films was far from perfect. Sometimes the sound would go "out of sync," the words failing to match the action. The comments of filmgoers with sensitive ears were probably on the lines

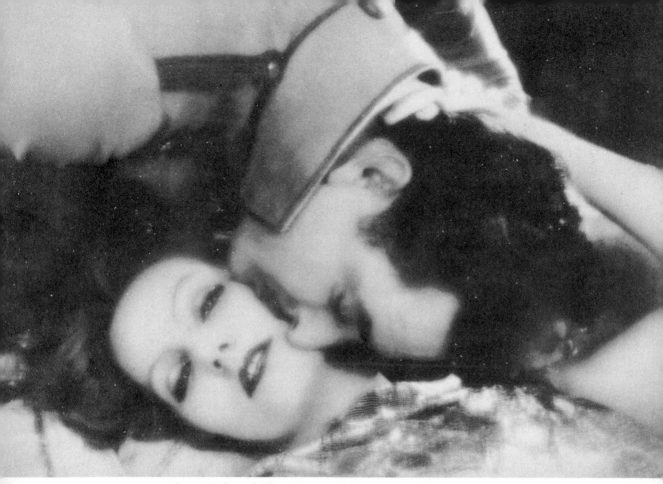

Greta Garbo and John Gilbert in The Flesh and the Devil

of Charles Chaplin's: The heroine seemed to be talking through sand, a door handle turning sounded like someone cranking up a farm tractor and a door closing like the collision of two lumber trucks. It was probably the shock of these sound effects to his sensibilities that influenced Chaplin to remain silent, a brilliantly expressive mime, in his future films, while other stars quacked, squeaked, and grated to the disillusionment of their fans.

Al Jolson jostled for popularity in 1928 with a very different star who might not be able to bring tears to all eyes by his rendering of "Mammy!" but who could certainly make millions laugh. He was Mickey Mouse, a cheerful little cartoon character first presented to the world by the film entrepreneur Walt Disney. Mickey, with his girl friend Minnie, became a general favourite in *Steamboat Willie* and *Plane Crazy*. On quite another plane the lovely Swedish actress Greta Garbo, who had been in films since 1922, was now heard in her characteristically deep, husky voice.

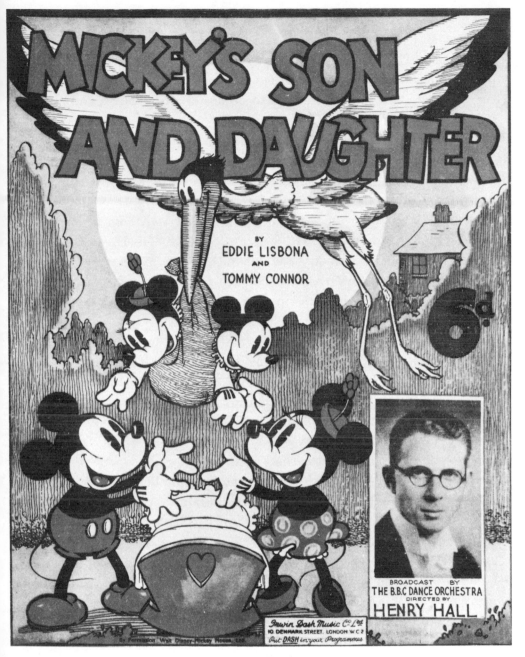

Mickey Mouse celebrated in song

Then came colour, with the musical spectacular *Rio Rita*, starring John Boles and Dolores Del Rio. It was crude, resembling hand-painted postcard artwork rather than nature, but it produced a sensation, and the black-and-white film began to look dull. It was the ambition of many pretty girls and good-looking young men to "get into the movies" regardless of acting talent, and many of them broke in, temporarily or permanently, including Georgina and the handsome footman Frederick, who had been James's batman in the war.

Musicals were flourishing in the theatre as well as the cinema. At Drury Lane there was *The Desert Song*, which would go on being performed by second-class and amateur companies up and down Britain until the original production had been long forgotten. It carried echoes of *The Sheik* and those steamy desert romances with which Ethel M. Dell had thrilled her readers. *The Vagabond King* at the Winter Garden introduced an unfamiliar figure to the stage—François Villon, fifteenth-century French poet and hell-raiser, involved in this piece in a fictitious romance with the Catherine de Vauçelles mentioned here and there in his poems. It gave London two notable melodies to hum, "Only a Rose" and "To Hell with Burgundy!" Another immortal, *Show Boat*, appeared in 1928, with the coloured actor Paul Robeson stopping the show with his singing of "Ol' Man River." During the run of the musical he gave some special matinee performances in which he introduced London to Negro spirituals.

The people who had been the Bright Young Things—toned down—were flocking to Noel Coward's revue *This Year of Grace*, which Coward had written—lyrics, music, and sketches—had largely produced, and in which he would star in New York, with the immensely funny Beatrice Lillie.

Serious music in London continued to be sustained by the long-established Queen's Hall Promenade Concerts under their conductor Sir Henry Wood. Control of them was taken over in 1927 by the BBC, no longer a company but established by royal charter as a corporation. Within five years the BBC's headquarters would have been moved from the old premises on the Embankment to a building that was looked on as the last word in architectural splendour, the liner-shaped Broadcasting House in Portland Place, at the end of Regent Street, next to the Queen's Hall itself.

So many books were being published in these years, by authors new and established, that only a few stand out vividly. J. B. Priestley's picaresque novel of a travelling concert party's adventures, *The Good Companions*, caught public fancy and became a best-seller, later turned into a play and a film starring the

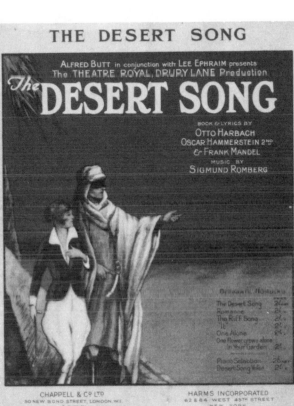

The covers of the sheet music for two enduring musicals

promising young actor John Gielgud. Richard Hughes's fantasy *A High Wind in Jamaica* caused a stir, as did Axel Munthe's *Story of San Michele* and Virginia Woolf's *Orlando*. Families like the Bellamys, not particularly given to what was known as "highbrow" reading, would probably dip into them out of curiosity, and they would be in demand from public and other lending libraries, as would Margaret Kennedy's novel *The Constant Nymph,* with its touching young heroine and her musician lover Lewis Dodd, which had been popularized in a stage version starring, once again, the ubiquitous Noel Coward.

Author D. H. Lawrence

Una Lady Troubridge (left) and novelist Radclyffe Hall

Sculptor Jacob Epstein

But, Upstairs and Downstairs, two books that could not fail to be discussed, though not read, appeared in 1928. For years D. H. Lawrence had been shocking his critics by his outspoken treatment of sex in his novels and poems. One novel had been suppressed for indecency, and some of the poems, posted from abroad, were referred to the extremely narrow-minded Home Secretary, Sir William Joynson-Hicks, known, not very affectionately, as "Jix." He passed them on to the Director of Public Prosecutions. But this was as nothing compared with the storm raised by Lawrence's novel *Lady Chatterley's Lover*, dealing in some detail and uninhibited language with the amours of a titled lady and her virile gamekeeper. It was published in Italy, but rumours and copies of it got back to England and raised a storm of outrage. An expurgated edition was published in 1932, but smuggled volumes of the original continued to be read in plain covers.

Also in 1928 a novel by the woman novelist Radclyffe Hall, called *The Well of Loneliness* and dealing with the forbidden subject of lesbianism, caused such an outcry that the police took action against it.

Literature was not the only art to come in for scandalized criticism. The "school" of painting indiscriminately known as Cubist, Futurist, or Surrealist aroused intense loathing among conventionally minded art lovers who had been reared on the popular paintings of Millais and the representational, often sentimental, pictures of the earlier years of the century. They viewed with horror portraits composed of lines and squares, the human form portrayed in impossible attitudes and with distorted limbs and features. Pictures that would one day change hands for tens of thousands of pounds were lampooned. Paul Klee's "A Young Girl" aroused the comment, "One of the maxims of Modern Art must be: Take your money in advance and then be as rude as you like to the sitter." Suzanne Roger's "Le Lac," showing two female nudes in landscape, appeared to a critic likely to be "intended to represent two women vainly endeavouring to boil a kettle on an old kitchen stove."

Sculpture came in for some hard knocks. In 1925 Jacob Epstein's memorial to W. H. Hudson was installed in the bird sanctuary of Kensington Gardens— appropriately, it was thought, because it represented Rima, the bird girl in Hudson's novel *Green Mansions*. But the sculptor's evident vision of mysterious beauty was not appreciated by the public, who found the flat-faced, large-handed stone lady with her hair complicated by birds repulsive and ludicrous. She was attacked not only verbally but with paint and missiles, and the protests she aroused would only be surpassed by the unveiling of Epstein's giant pregnant figure "Genesis" in 1931.

Such works of art were emblematic of the enormous changes in freedom of style since the days when Lady Marjorie had been alive and James and Elizabeth still young. There were plenty of Victorians around to resist them. "Jix" himself had been born in 1865.

More to the popular taste, as the Twenties drew to their close, were the Kewpie (Cupid) dolls to be won on fairgrounds, fat celluloid babies with a single, beribboned lock of hair. Dolls were very much in fashion, not only with children. As, in Victorian times, the legs of chairs and pianos had been discreetly draped, so the telephones of the late Twenties were covered by the skirts of large, often beautiful "crinoline" dolls, sometimes in Georgian powdered hair and costume, sometimes modishly shingled. The same type of doll would form a lady's nightdress or pyjama case (pyjamas were now all the rage among young women), and smaller versions would top pincushions and face-powder bowls. Sometimes the head would be of a Pierrot, a cult figure of the day. Georgina's dressing table would contain some such item and a scent spray of crystal or decorated porcelain, with a squeeze bulb attached—the precursor of the push-button spray. Her nightwear would be expensive and beautiful, garments of chiffon, silk, and lace; it had taken centuries for the high-necked nightdress of flannel to disappear, but it was finally dead. Even Rose, Ruby, and Daisy would wear pretty night attire, from the new stores that were opening everywhere in London.

New houses were going up, too, very much on the lines of the ones built just after the war. The larger ones, intended for, perhaps, civil servants and the professional classes, would be advertised as having "bed-sitting-room for maid." The maid would be far better accommodated than the servants at No. 165 had been; she would have more freedom, would treat her employers less deferentially. Her work would be easier, with so many labour-saving appliances and the increased use of electric and gas fires, and there would probably be a charwoman who would come in daily to do the rough work. No housewife of any social status would expect to run her house and her family single-handed. A romantic story of 1928 refers to a young woman living in a small country cottage as having a "day-girl," presumably because she would not have stooped to keep it clean herself. Another story, of 1927, is set in a house in the imaginary Seymour Gardens, on the edge of Hyde Park. It is, presumably, nothing like the size of 165 Eaton Place, for it is owned by a widower with no family. Yet his staff includes "Elsie, the under-housemaid," which implies that a house-parlourmaid was also kept, and a butler, Mr. Beldon, whose wife is the cook. Evidently by this date the old rule by which butlers must not be married had been relaxed, and Mr. Hudson could, if he had wished it, have married Mrs. Bridges and kept his situation.

These better-type houses, and often smaller ones, would have garages. To keep a car was a definite status symbol; there were many who not only did not own a car but had never even ridden in one and regarded such a ride as a great

Pedestrian (to reckless driver): "D-don't kill me—I'm on my way to buy a car . . . so . . . I'll soon be on your side!"

treat. The comfortably housed and privileged maid in the middle-class home might have a boy friend who was doing well, but when they eventually married the possession of a car would not only not be on their list of priorities; it simply would not occur to them. The Great Car Joke—and there were many— invariably referred to sporty young couples or prosperous middle-aged ones. *Punch* abounded with them. One such drawing shows an elegant car broken down in a country lane, the driver (plus-foured) under the bonnet desperately trying to make it start, while his wife mildly surveys his efforts. The caption is: "Enid [in her best furs]: 'Can I help you, dearest?'" In another picture a car has come to grief in a hedge. The Fair Passenger, thrown out into a field and looking much the worse for wear, stretches out her gloved hand in the grass. "Oh, Reggie, look! The first primrose!" The Lady Driver Joke was already a favourite. One of them is shown turning round from the driving seat to her husband, who is frantically pushing the car from behind. "I'm learning quite a lot about driving, sitting here, George. I've just found out how to put on the brakes."

Even with prices incredibly low, by today's standards, the cost of living was gradually mounting. Said Denis Mackail, writing as early as 1927:

One reads a lot of stuff nowadays about the breaking up of big estates, and the turning of big houses into hotels, and the disappearance of the old order of things under the crushing load of taxation.

One also gathers, from a casual inspection of the contemporary Press, that the only people who have any money left today are the Americans and the unemployed; that the idle rich have all become the hard-working poor; that everyone who used to live in the country now lives in London; and that they might just as well have stayed where they were, seeing that steel houses, broadcasting, and arterial roads have reduced our native land to one vast, monotonous level, inhabited by a debt-ridden population who are waiting in dull apathy for complete extermination in the next war.

He was looking on the dark side, as he went on to say, pointing out that in the hunting shires one still met rich people on expensive horses following the hounds. But, in fact, a slow revolution was going on. After the death of the Dowager Countess it is unlikely that Southwold, the country seat, remained in the Bellamy family. Unless it was bought by one of the tycoons who had made a fortune out of armaments after the war and had held on to it, the house would probably be turned into a country hotel or possibly become a hospital or similar institution. In those days when pulmonary tuberculosis struck down so many, convalescent homes in the country were much in demand.

As for 165 Eaton Place, there would come a day when it became too expensive for the Bellamy family to run. Like so many other once-grand houses in Belgravia and Mayfair, it would be turned into apartments, its huge drawing room divided into sections to provide several rooms instead of one. The garage, once a stable, with the flat above it where Edward and Daisy lived, would become a single unit, one of the mews houses which in the Thirties would be an ultra-smart living accommodation. London was changing rapidly. Piccadilly was losing its great houses from which the aristocracy had gazed across the carriage road to the Green Park. Devonshire House, where the beautiful Duchess Georgiana of Gainsborough's portrait had lived in a strange *ménage à trois*, had been demolished and replaced by a nine-storey block of shops and luxury flats. The face of Piccadilly Circus had been changed by the opening of the Piccadilly Tube Station. Park Lane, once the most elegant street in London, lost Dorchester House and Grosvenor House, both being replaced by vast, unlovely hotels, while other houses were turned over to commercial uses.

Belgravia itself would be demoted. By 1931 a row of Georgian houses would have given way to the vast Victoria Coach Station, and the grimy tentacles of Victoria Station would gradually extend towards Eaton Place. Shops, restaurants, lodging houses, and apartments took over what had been solely residential. Gardens disappeared under bricks and mortar. The noble houses of Eaton Square and Belgrave Square (where at the Southwolds' townhouse Mrs. Bridges had applied for the job that introduced her into the Bellamy family) became government offices and embassies. The days of the one-family, one-house arrangement were virtually over in fashionable London by 1930.

Signs of the times in 1929 could be seen one day in Trafalgar Square, to which unemployed Glasgow workers had made a hunger march. The Great Depression of 1929–1931 was making itself felt. Haggard faces under cloth caps would appear frequently in the 1930s, wearily marching to London in an attempt to

Workers on a hunger march

Women voters seeking information

bring pressure to bear upon the government. In five years as Prime Minister Stanley Baldwin had found no real answer to the recurring problems of falling exports and idle industries. Unemployment was rife and was the main ground on which the 1929 election was fought. Three parties contested it, including the Liberal Party, which was greatly diminished but fought on under Lloyd George and proposed drastic campaigns to conquer the problems. Ramsay MacDonald, the Labour leader, issued a manifesto promising wholescale nationalization and heavy taxes on the rich. Stanley Baldwin, the plodding, earnest, and ineffectual man who seemed to be happiest in the country among his books, stuck to the unprogressive slogan "Safety First!"

He lost the election, and Richard Bellamy's party went out of power. The electorate was the biggest ever to have voted. For the first time all women had the right to vote, and a woman, Margaret Bondfield, as Minister of Labour, became the first woman to attain Cabinet rank. Hopes were high that things might change for the better, especially when, in the summer of 1929, the serious illness of King George cleared up in the healthful surroundings of Bognor on the Sussex coast. His gratitude took the form of bestowing the title Regis on the little town, and a ceremony of thanksgiving was held at Westminster Abbey, where the frail figure of the King was greeted by loyal, cheering crowds. Whatever the government, the monarchy held its own in the affections of the people.

In October came the blow that would affect the Bellamy family fortunes. The industrial boom in the United States, ever-growing since the end of the war, suddenly ended with the collapse of the Wall Street stock market. The tide of ruin spread, even beyond the Atlantic. Germany had overcome her difficulties

Liberal Party election headquarters

In 1930 the way was open for Nazism.

and stabilized herself during the Twenties, but the Wall Street crash rocked her, causing a vast wave of unemployment that carried her youth towards Hitler and his National Socialist Party. The way was open for Nazism.

In 1930 the great British racing driver Henry Segrave was killed while breaking the water speed record for the second time in his boat *Miss England II*, travelling at 100 miles an hour on Lake Windermere. The airship R 101 crashed during her flight to India. Britain, never anxious to be downhearted if there were any alternative, read the ominous headlines and then applied itself to sport and pastimes. One could go "hiking" with troops of other energetic young and not-so-young people in jerseys, shorts, ankle socks, and rucksacks over the blessedly unbuilt-on countryside. It was the first time people had ever walked in company for pleasure. Pantomime comedians appeared grotesquely got up as hikers; the song "I'm Happy When I'm Hiking" was heard everywhere. The novelist Hugh Walpole's *Herries Chronicle*, set in the Lake District, described scenery familiar to thousands who set off every weekend from the industrial North of England to enjoy the beauty and fresh air of the mountains. If it rained too much for outings, one could stay by the fire and do the crossword puzzle, which had become the indoor rage. So popular was it that *Punch*, in a cartoon called "The Ruling Passion," showed a gardener, laying out a new rose garden, enquiring of the owner, "Will ye 'ave standards across or down, sir?"

Sir Arthur Conan Doyle died in 1930, prematurely worn out by his tireless work for the cause of spiritualism. He had recently published a short story, "The

Weekend pleasures in the country

Disintegration Machine," in which an inventor who wished to sell a machine of terrible potential to "a certain foreign Power" was caught in his own net. Sherlock Holmes had made almost his last appearance in a competition set in the *Strand*, in which readers were invited to choose the best twelve of the famous stories. There was to be no resuscitation from the Reichenbach Falls for Holmes after 1930. Sir Arthur's conclusion to his address to the readers was not only poignant but apposite.

And so, reader, farewell to Sherlock Holmes! I thank you for your constancy, and can but hope that some return has been made in the shape of that distraction from the worries of life and stimulating change of thought which can only be found in the fairy kingdom of romance.

How would London seem, if we could return to it, in this last year when the Bellamys and their servants were to be found at 165 Eaton Place? Its traffic would be restfully less than our own, with plenty of horses still drawing vans. The London air would be less polluted by fumes, but in winter the thick yellow fog known as "London particular" would come down and obscure the city in the choking haze familiar to Holmes and Watson. Servants like Ruby would still be seen going on errands to the many small shops which would later be swept away. We would be struck by the fact that everybody, without exception, wore a hat. Not until the Thirties would the "hatless brigade" be predominant. We would find that the first names used in our society among people who have only just met would have been thought disgracefully informal. Those dwellers in the pseudo-Tudor, semidetached houses that then ringed London in every direction would be Mr. and Mrs. to their neighbours, not Mary and John; only in the theatre world would the exchange of first names be the accepted thing. We would have been able to see the first production of *Private Lives* at the Phoenix Theatre, with Noel Coward, the author, as Elyot Chase and the delightful "Gertie" Lawrence as Amanda Prynne, and at the Adelphi the stunningly pretty Jessie Matthews in Benn Levy's *Evergreen*, the story of a young actress pretending to be her own mother miraculously rejuvenated.

Radio was still so much the accepted entertainment of the masses that people would shut themselves in with the lights out and the curtains drawn, in order not to be disturbed by callers when some favourite programme was being broadcast. When they went to bed, the large majority of people would do so by the light of a candle; electric light in the house was usually confined to one light

"The very poor . . . slept along the Embankment on benches. . . ."

in the middle of the ceiling. The elderly, in the lower and middle classes, might have a bath in the house but would be suspicious of using it, and if they did use it, it would not be more than once a week. Their tastes, standards, habits would all be revolutionized by television, which in 1930 had its programmes advertised for the first time in the *Daily Express*.

Londoners were singing and whistling whatever tune they had just heard broadcast or used in a film—"Broadway Melody," "Blue Moon," "Singing in the Rain." They sounded, and looked, on the whole a good deal more cheerful and innocent than the Londoners of the 1970s, except for the very poor who slept along the Embankment on benches or performed pathetically tedious routines for the theatre queues sitting tidily on small canvas stools alongside the theatres. They were the people of the Twenties, who had been through so much and who, in spite of the newspapers' gloomy forebodings of a great slump, refused to believe that things would ever be so bad again as they had been. They were happily spared the knowledge of what the next decade, and the one after it, would bring to them and to London.

249

The past thirty years had wrought many changes in the lives of those who lived at 165 Eaton Place and in the lives of those in thousands of similar households. They were touched by the sadness and tragedies of their age: the death of Victoria and of Edward, the sinking of the *Titanic*, the Great War, and the passing of a romantic, genteel life-style never again to be enjoyed. They were affected, too, by the march of progress that was to change their lives as immutably as had the disasters. Radio, new forms of communication, the automobile, and the airplane shrank their world. The New Woman and the rise of the working class affected the social order. Nothing, however, did so much to mark the end of the age as did the Great Depression, which shook the establishment so violently that it virtually toppled from their high positions some of the wealthiest, most highly held members of London society. Among these were the Bellamys, who watched their fortune crumble with the stock-market crash. The day finally came when they, so long secure in their beautiful home surrounded by solicitous servants, watched their furniture carried out piece by piece from 165 Eaton Place, knowing that when the last piece had gone the familiar front door would shut them and their servants out forever.

As to the Bellamys, "they watched their furniture carried out piece by piece from 165 Eaton Place."

INDEX